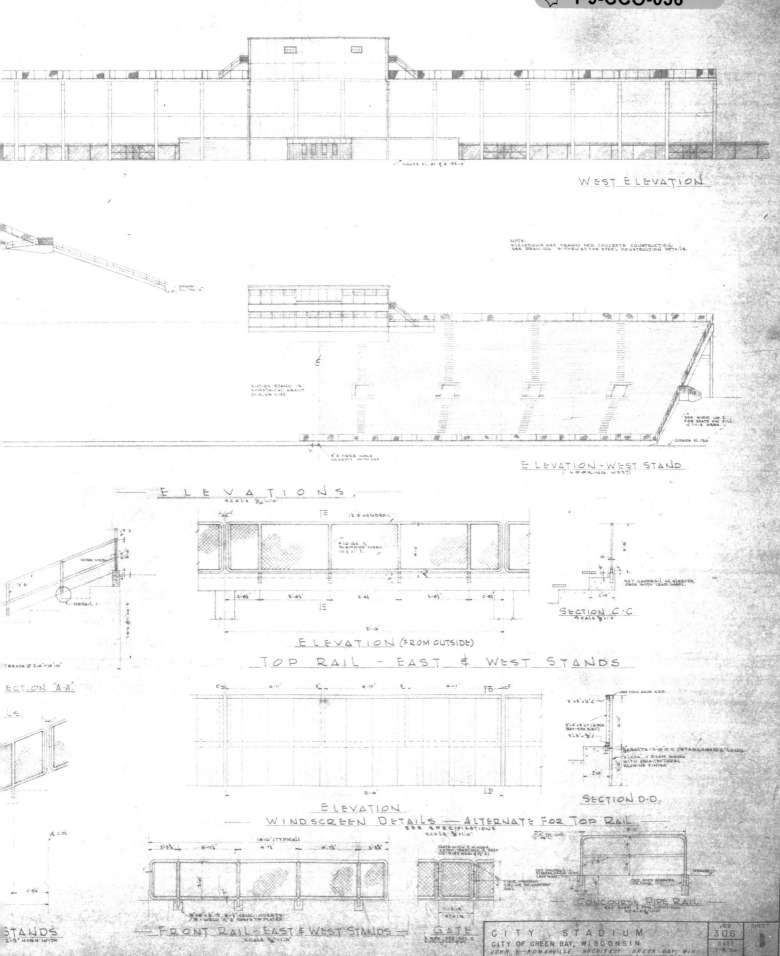

WEST ELEVATION

NOTE:
ELEVATIONS ARE DRAWN FOR CONCRETE CONSTRUCTION.
SEE DRAWING 51 THRU 67 FOR STEEL CONSTRUCTION DETAILS.

ELEVATION - WEST STAND
(LOOKING WEST)

ELEVATIONS

ELEVATION (FROM OUTSIDE)

TOP RAIL - EAST & WEST STANDS

SECTION C-C

SECTION A-A

ELEVATION

WINDSCREEN DETAILS — ALTERNATE FOR TOP RAIL

SECTION D-D

FRONT RAIL - EAST & WEST STANDS

GATE

CONCOURSE PIPE RAIL

CITY STADIUM
CITY OF GREEN BAY, WISCONSIN
JOHN E. SOMERVILLE, ARCHITECT   GREEN BAY, WIS.

JOB 306

THE PACKERS!

Steve Cameron

Bob Snodgrass
Coordinating Consultant

Dan Hill
Commemorative Specialist

Jack Smith
Fine Books Specialist

Vernon Biever
Photo Editor

Chuck Carlson
Researcher

Anita Stumbo
Design and Typography

Packer Memorabilia courtesy John Des Jardins
Production Assistance by Debra Weld, Stacie Masterson, Russ Reaver,
   Kim Gates, Ginger Stallings, Jerry Steely, Michael Zahn
Fiber Optic photo Wolf Photography and Chris Dennis
Dust Jacket photo by Vernon Biever
Dust Jacket Design by John Martin and Bonnie Henson
Hall of Fame Gatefold art and photos courtesy
   ProFootball Hall of Fame
Endsheet Stadium Drawings courtesy John E. Sommerville
Contributing Photographers: Vernon Biever, John Biever, Rod Hanna,
   Steve Smart, Chris Vleisides, Harmann Studios, Dave Garot
Early Era photos courtesy Stiller and LeFebvre Collections
Select photos courtesy Packer Hall of Fame, Green Bay Press Gazette and
   Milwaukee Sentinel
Remaining photos courtesy the Green Bay Packers
Original artwork courtesy Michael Duane

Published by Taylor Publishing Company, Dallas, Texas

ISBN: 0–87833–046–1 (General)
ISBN: 0–87833–047–x (Limited)
ISBN: 0–87833–048–8 (Collectors)

For those special friends from way back who stuck and stayed before there were any books. They know who they are.

And for Jeffrey Michael Flanagan, who is not only an Oshkosh kid and lifetime Packer fan, but who did the impossible — restoring my faith in young sportswriters.

About the Author

Steve Cameron has been covering pro football and assorted other sports for a quarter-century. He has been a beat reporter, columnist and feature writer for newspapers in several cities, in addition to contributing regularly to major magazines and other periodicals.

Winner of numerous awards for overall sports writing and works on subjects as varied as greyhound racing, basketball on the Navajo reservation and train trips around America with coach-turned-broadcaster John Madden, Cameron also edited a golf guide to the Caribbean which was published in 1983. He is the author of *Moments, Memories and Miracles,* a 25-year chronicle of the Kansas City Royals baseball franchise released by Taylor Publishing Company in 1992.

A native San Franciscan whose father was one of the 49ers' first accountants when that team was formed in 1946, Cameron now lives in Arizona, where he is a sports columnist and radio commentator.

*A Salute to the Past
and a
Commitment to the Future*

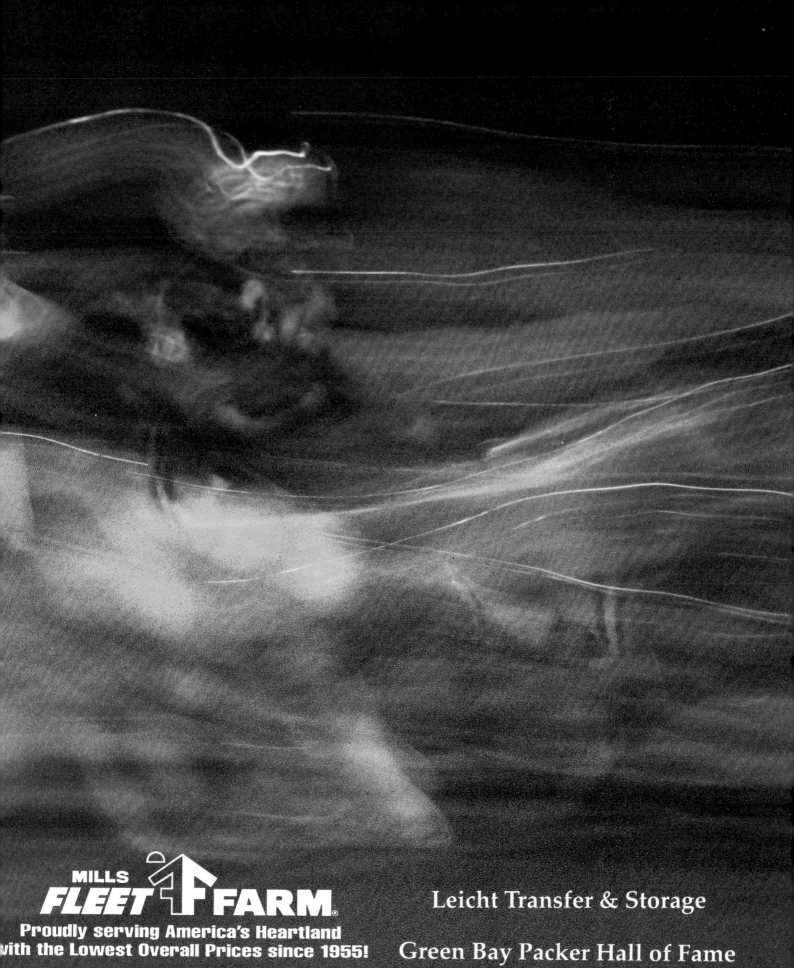

Contents

Acknowledgments

Researching and writing a book on a franchise as successful as the Green Bay Packers is a staggering enterprise.

That's the word for it: staggering.

Seventy-five seasons. Eleven world championships. Hundreds of magnificent players. This was the kind of task to make an author survey the situation and say, "My God, where do I start?"

The only way is with lots and lots of help, believe me.

I'm indebted, first of all, to the Packer organization itself and all the wonderful people there — and throughout the Green Bay area — who warmed to this project with so much gusto. And offered cooperation above and beyond any reasonable call of duty.

It's easy to see why the football world believes this legendary franchise may be on the verge of another magnificent era. Executives like Packers president Bob Harlan and general manager Ron Wolf are the sort of folks who always do things well, and they were both kind and forthcoming as we put the 75th anniversary celebration into book form.

So was coach Mike Holmgren, but of course, I knew that going in. We've been neighbors a couple of times in our lives without ever knowing it. You can always count on a homeboy.

Public relations guru Lee Remmel is a treasure. Besides his official capacity as keeper of records, pictures and other Packer artifacts, Lee has this incredible memory for facts, figures and anecdotes that is simply beyond belief. His single weakness, best I can see, is that he's not so hot giving a newcomer street directions. But that's OK, Lee, I enjoyed that tour of Door County while searching for the Green Bay public library.

Oh, one more thing about Mr. Remmel: It has to be mentioned that he helped babysit our book at perhaps the busiest, most chaotic time he's had in years. Here were the Packers signing guys like Reggie White — with the requisite press conferences and general hubbub — and Lee still managed to squeeze in time to help. While juggling the demands of the draft and mini-camp, as well. I can't even imagine doing it without him.

Nor without Lee's assistant, Jeff Blumb, who helped keep an eye on everything and gave this manuscript a thorough, professional reading.

Actually, you can say the same thing for so many others inside the organization. Coaches, staff members, film guys — they were all great.

What could I possibly add to the work of photographer Vernon Biever, who must have printed about a million pictures for us to sift through? Do not visit Vernon's home, for your own sake. There are so many thrilling images stored there, it's almost impossible to leave.

It's no accident that this book is attractive: Vernon, the other photographers who contributed, designer Anita Stumbo, artists John Martin and Michael Duane all have gained reputations for crackerjack work and they lived up to their billing.

This is my second time around working on a major project with the movers and shakers from Taylor Publishing Company, so I have to admit that while I'm mightily impressed with their skills, I wasn't surprised. They're just doggone good and they'll keep on being good.

Bob Snodgrass, Dan Hill and drawlin' Jack Smith down in Dallas are getting to be buddies as well as colleagues, and that is definitely my gain. Bob is even pretending to endure my cigars — not necessarily liking them, you understand, but coming around to serious patience. There's a special place in heaven for you, Robert.

Thanks, many times over, to Chuck Carlson of the *Appleton Post-Crescent*, who acted as researcher and general handyman putting the book together. Chuck is working on a book of his own now. I hope he remembers me when he's rich and famous and doing the network talk shows.

So many others around Green Bay and the state of Wisconsin deserve a nod, including all the smiling staff at the Marriott Residence Inn who kept me comfortable — and halfway sane — and certainly folks like Pat O'Connell, Kelly Schiltz and Jim Van Matre at the Packer Hall of Fame, who opened up their wonders to us and made sure we found what we needed.

I won't forget all the neat folks at Fox Valley Greyhound Park for creating some fine off-hours entertainment, either. Or the Green Bay Pizza Company, for delivering on time. I never knew you could find big-time pizza in Brown County.

Needless to say, there couldn't be any 75th anniversary book without the Packers themselves, and I owe a great debt to all the current and former players who took the time to re-live their own special memories. I could sit and talk for hours to guys like Ray Nitschke and Fuzzy Thurston.

One amazing aspect of putting this thing together is that so many books already have been done on the Packers, particularly from the Lombardi era. These were invaluable tools, and we would not have the same flavor and authenticity without them.

This is just a partial list of the books we used to gather 75 years worth of information: *Lombardi!*, by John Wiebusch; *Instant Replay* and *Distant Replay*, by Jerry Kramer with Dick Schaap; *Run to Daylight*, by Vince Lombardi with W.C. Heinz; *Mean on Sunday*, by Ray Nitschke with Robert Wells; *Starr*, by Bart Starr with Murray Olderman; *The Packer Legend*, by John B. Torinus; and *Packer Legends in Facts*, by Eric Goska.

Various other accounts — in newspapers, magazines and assorted publications — were likewise critical to assembling the big picture. There's no way I could name every source here, but all those involved rate my deepest gratitude.

And finally, thanks again to my own personal support group — those special friends who seem to have jump-started a career in the book-writing business — particularly Mike Patrick and Becca Rothschild, for studiously editing the manuscript. Any mistake left standing is mine, not theirs.

Old pal Tim Keithley came through one more time with a cozy place to stay and our regular supply of Pop-Tarts. Jeff Flanagan offered a desk in his sumptuous new home so I'd have a place to land my flying computer. Naturally, the ever-understanding Janet Freeman and everyone else back in Arizona who fed my growing brood of cats or kept my spirits up when battle fatigue seemed imminent — well, they all deserve a medal.

Nothing less. Ain't it fun, gang?

— S.C.

Foreword

To me, the Green Bay Packer "story" is endlessly fascinating. It is unique in all of professional sports, and always will be, because it cannot be duplicated. No longer is it possible for a city the size of Green Bay (pop. 97, 801) to have and support a major league franchise in any professional sport, a fact which makes the Packer story all the more remarkable.

This being our 75th season, it seemed the perfect time to update this intriguing story in book form — a story of a team which, surviving a number of major financial crises along the way — has won more championships (eleven) than any other in the annals of professional football and remains the only one ever to have won three consecutive titles.

The how and why Green Bay succeeded — where many another "small town" fell by the wayside in the National Football League's early and formative years — makes great reading. I am confident that the contributions and exploits of such memorable "names" as Curly Lambeau, Vince Lombardi, Don Hutson, Willie Davis and Paul Hornung — and such climactic moments as Bart Starr's celebrated sneak for the winning touchdown in the "Ice Bowl" — will come alive for you in the pages of *The Packers! Seventy-five Seasons of Memories and Mystique in Green Bay.*

Robert E. Harlan

Robert E. Harlan
President and CEO
Green Bay Packers

Introduction

Like so many men who reach that indeterminate age when sports participation becomes whittled down to golf and slow-pitch softball, I suffer from fairly chronic low back pain.

This can't have a connection to the Packers, you say. Oh, but it does.

For one thing, back trouble is not a good thing for an author.

Sitting stiffly over a computer keyboard is tolerable for the time it takes to whip through a column, game story or most other newspaper assignments, but a full-size book takes hours, days, weeks and more of scrunched-up concentration.

For whatever reason — I could blame the Wisconsin weather but other, sturdier folk seem to bear it pretty well — discomfort came with a vengeance during that intense stretch when we were putting together this volume on the Packers. There is no escaping a deadline, however, so I took pills on command and shuttled into hot baths and over to the whirlpool whenever possible. And then back to the work table.

One weekend was particularly miserable. In fact, my back seized up so frightfully that I had to walk around almost doubled over while pursuing interviews at the Pack's spring mini-camp.

The only obvious recourse was rest. Take a few days — maybe even a week — and let the spasms subside. That was the prudent thing, the wise move, but I never did it.

Remember now, to research this book I spent hundreds of hours immersed in Packer lore — which a lot of the time meant reading and hearing about Vince Lombardi. If you can be overpowered by a man more than two decades after his passing, well, that's what happened to me.

When you are around the Packers — then, now, anytime — you tend to come back again and again to Lombardi. And doggone it, all I could think of when that relentless ache returned to my lower spine was Lombardi's oft-repeated axiom about playing hurt.

"Pain is in the mind," he told his athletes. "If you can walk, you can run. And if you can run, you can play."

So I played. Coach Lombardi won another one.

Amazing things happen when you edge up close to the Packers, though. I decided, for instance, that one of the first items on the agenda when I arrived in Green Bay would be to visit Lambeau Field, walk onto that famous turf and head straight to the south end zone. I wanted to see the very spot where Bart Starr slammed into a frozen mass of bodies on the final play of the historic Ice Bowl — the NFL championship game of December 31, 1967.

I wanted to get a sense of the event, to imagine the thunderous collision of frostbitten warriors, to actually feel Jerry Kramer and Kenny Bowman laying just enough block on Dallas tackle Jethro Pugh that Starr could wedge himself over the goal line beneath the savage leap of linebacker Chuck Howley.

The famous "frozen tundra" was soft the day of my pilgrimage — you could hardly ask for a minus-46 wind chill just for old times' sake — but yes, the ghosts were there. Weather aside, anyone with a sense of football history almost certainly would feel a little chill standing on that particular patch of grass.

Come to find out, my notion of somehow recreating the moment for the sake of research was hardly unique. It turns out that whenever there is a Packer fantasy camp — you know, one of those outings for diehard fans who'll do anything to put on the uniform of their favorite team — the highlight always comes down at the south end zone. One fantasy camper after another takes the football and dives over, keeping the Ice Bowl alive today as though it happened last season instead of a quarter-century ago.

Packers president Bob Harlan claims he sees the same phenomenon all the time, and not just relating to one title game, either.

"Whenever we play at home, I usually try to make sure I'm watching when the visiting team gets to the stadium," Harlan said. "You know how, before the guys go into the locker room to get taped and put on all their gear, they'll always walk out on the field?

"Players do it everywhere they go. Just walk around, check out the grass or AstroTurf and get a feel. But when they come to Green Bay, it's different. You can see them staring. These are players now, not fans. I always notice how they look up at the names of all the great Packer Hall of Famers and then they look at all the championship seasons, all those numbers painted at the top of the stadium.

"Every time I see that, it reminds me what an incredibly special place this is."

Hall of Fame broadcaster Ray Scott (left) always has insisted the Packers stay in your heart for life — and he's right.

Actually, it's impossible to forget Green Bay's unique niche in the football firmament. Consider: I set up a meeting with legendary linebacker Ray Nitschke, and we agreed to meet in the lobby of the downtown Holiday Inn. The day came up cold, windy and rain-swept — the type of afternoon that keeps folks' heads down and attention riveted to getting home to that nice, warm fire.

It was an off hour, too, well past the time there would be any crowd in the hotel restaurant for lunch. The place was nearly deserted and whatever staff was around seemed to have disappeared into offices or assorted other cubbyholes. But when Nitschke arrived — with his jacket collar turned up against the cold and a ball cap pulled low on his forehead — he was instantly recognized by a small swarm of people who hadn't even been visible moments earlier.

Everyone wanted an autograph. For aunts, uncles, a cousin over in Eau Claire. Please, Ray, sign this one to so-and-so and this one for my sister. Slips of paper began flying around like confetti.

I thought: This is unbelievable. Here's a man who hasn't played football since 1972. Nitschke said: "There's no way to explain how these people love the Packers. You just have to experience it for yourself. There's nothing like it anywhere else and there never will be."

True enough.

In mid-1993, the Packers announced the celebration of their 75th anniversary — dating back to August 11, 1919, when Curly Lambeau and local sports editor George Whitney Calhoun dreamed up a football team over a stein of beer. Current club public relations director Lee Remmel alerted the area media that there would be a short, informal press conference at the stadium to unveil the anniversary logo, discuss selection of an all-time Packer team and so forth.

This is the sort of function which might draw a handful of people elsewhere, but in Green Bay they came in number — all the writers, radio guys with recorders, cameras from every TV station, even columnist Bud Lea up from Milwaukee. I'm thinking: All this to see a patch that will be sewn on uniform sleeves?

In the course of that press gathering, Remmel also mentioned that a commemorative book was in the works and, lo and behold, I was summoned before the crowd. An author whom most present had never met, a fellow who had yet to write a word of this much-awaited volume, and still cameras whirred and reporters scribbled.

If I had any doubt that I had arrived in the one true football capital of America, it was surely dispelled that evening when I saw my face and heard my words on the evening news — suggesting that the only way to approach a book on the Green Bay Packers was with a deep sense of awe.

E.L. (Curly) Lambeau–Founder, player, coach & vice-president

Bart Starr

Vince Lombardi

Ray Nitschke

John Jefferson

James Lofton

Tony Canadeo

Don Hutson

Sterling Sharpe

Mike Holmgren

Lambeau Field capacity: 56,926

Willie Wood

Herb Adderley

Paul Hornung

Lynn Dickey

Brett Favre

Johnny (Blood) McNally

Arnie Herber

Willie Davis

Jim Ringo

Reggie White

Mike Michalske

Robert (Cal) Hubbard

Clarke Hinkle

The Packer Sweep

Bart Starr hands off to Jim Taylor who follows Jerry Kramer & Fuzzy Thurston

Forrest Gregg

John Brockington

Michael Dubois

And with that awe comes responsibility. I've tried very hard to do the Packer mystique justice, but trust me, it's a daunting task. So many championships, so many heroes, so much history. Not to mention an intensity of feeling that can't possibly exist between a team and a town — even an entire state — anywhere else in sports.

What I've attempted to do is capture as much as possible of the Packers' staggering story, yet keep it in context and blend it in with the here and now. There is very definitely a feeling these days that the Pack at last is back, that the current regime led by general manager Ron Wolf and coach Mike Holmgren will return Green Bay onto what the good burghers in these parts believe is the Packers' rightful throne.

"The fans here are incredibly loyal, but above all they're patient," Harlan said. "There are so many families who have been here a long time that stories about great Packer teams from other eras get passed down. Sometimes I think the young ones kind of expect that it's just about time for the next Packer dynasty."

And why not?

After three decades of almost nonstop success under team founder Lambeau, these people endured a decade and a half of losing teams until Lombardi arrived to set it all right.

Now there's a sense it's all happening again but — yea or nay — they'll still love the Packers with a passion that reminds you more of family than a typical city-team relationship.

"The feeling for the Packers in Green Bay and all around Wisconsin — and from people all over the country — is just different than anything else you'll see," said Fuzzy Thurston, the longtime offensive guard who stayed on as proprietor of local restaurants and saloons. "I'm just like everybody else now, too. I get so excited at the games I go to the bathroom more often than the players. Sometimes I can't even watch because I'm afraid a play won't work."

Thurston is hardly alone in his loyalty. It's one thing for the general public to root for a team, especially when times are good. But here, you find former players almost unanimous in professing an unbroken passion for the Packers. And of course, those thousands of others who turn up — whether it's 30 degrees or 30 below — are unflinching with their devotion.

This book is for those fans.

It's nothing more than my personal belief — but a strong one — that readers enjoy a book on the team they care about much more if it isn't presented, as many are, as simple history. Most of the time, whether the occasion is 25 years, or 75, or 100, these things turn into history books. They start at day one and proceed chronologically to the present.

Nothing wrong with that, I suppose, for a classroom setting. But I'm a fan, too, and I don't think that's the way folks remember things. If a gang of Packer loyalists gathers in a barber shop, pancake house or tavern and someone begins telling yarns, they don't open the conversation by talking about 1919 and finally finish with '93. No offense to history profs or people who put together encyclopedias, but that's just not how it is.

I've tried here to put the Packer saga into a package that's not just a look at the whole glorious run, but as a story fans will find fun to read. It's not arranged year by year, for instance. In fact, it starts with a peek at Green Bay itself, which seems appropriate because the legend never could have developed as it has anywhere but in this one particular hard-working, rock-solid community in northeastern Wisconsin.

No way.

After that, the book works backward and then forward again, which sounds sort of strange but when you read it, hopefully you'll see why that's the best way to tell the amazing Packer story.

Perhaps some of your own favorite memories may be left out or given a little less attention than you think they deserve. That's certainly possible, since the Packers claim so many serious devotees and there have been momentous events so numerous they could fill several bound editions. My goodness, there has been enough literature devoted to the Pack over the years to fill a small library.

While cramming for such a challenging assignment as squeezing that history into a book concise enough that it wouldn't have to be hauled about by a team of mules, I read and often re-read more than a million words on this team.

So in the end, I did my best — to make it complete and make it exciting.

And accurate. Sometimes there are various versions of the same tale floating around, so that precise reporting is almost impossible. Everyone's heard the story about Lombardi announcing to All-Pro center Jim Ringo that he'd been traded — simply because Ringo brought

an agent in to discuss his contract. Exactly what Ringo said and how Lombardi replied has been pounded around on the banquet circuit — I've read about four different conversations, all similar but no two precisely the same.

The point, I guess, is to capture the flavor of the thing.

Max McGee has offered up contradictory accounts about what he did the night before his remarkable performance in Super Bowl I. Was he tucked in bed or out on the town in Los Angeles? Did he really make all those circus catches without a wink of sleep or did Max, a wonderful yarn-spinner and hail fellow well met by anyone's standards, create a little fiction that fit with his playboy reputation?

It doesn't matter. This book is about capturing the essence of the Packers and the people who have made the franchise so unique. Readers get to fill in some of their own blanks, and that's part of the enjoyment.

Many years ago, I wound up by chance as a golf-tournament partner of Ray Scott, a broadcaster for the ages but also the man who became known to America as the voice of the Packers during the Lombardi era. We've kept in touch a long time, Ray and I, and when the agreement was struck for me to do a 75th anniversary recap, I phoned him.

"As a writer, you'll be swept up in it," Ray said. "I recall so well something Willie Davis said when somebody asked him — years after his career was over — about Lombardi. Willie said: 'There isn't a day that goes by that I don't think of that man.'

"That's the way I feel about the Packers. And you will, too."

I believe you're right, Ray.

Steve Cameron
Green Bay, Wisconsin
July 1993

32,132 Jam Packers' New Home

Nixon Praises
Green Bay Fans

MILWAUKEE SENTINEL

**Little Rock Editor
Puts Guilt on Faubus**

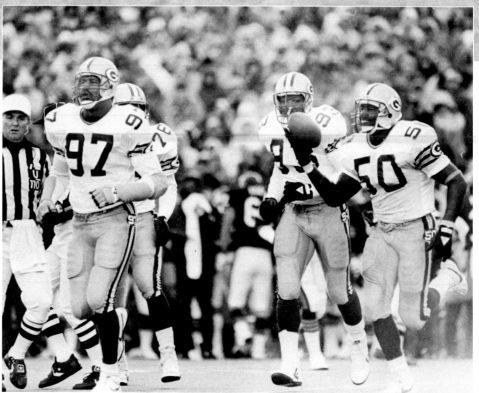

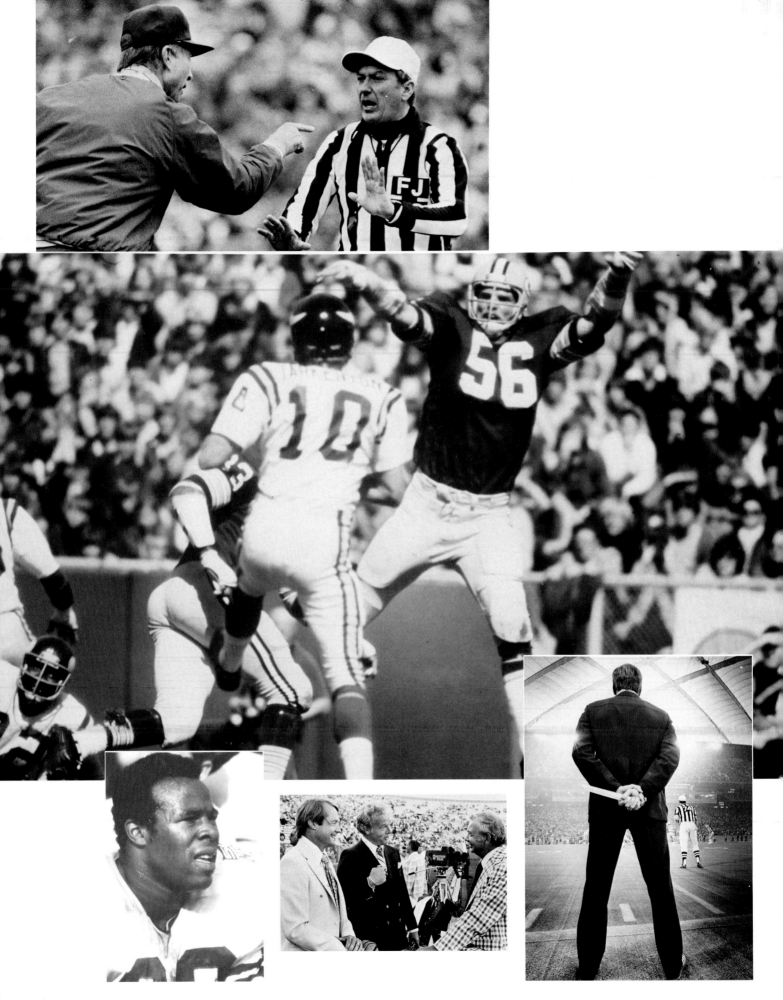

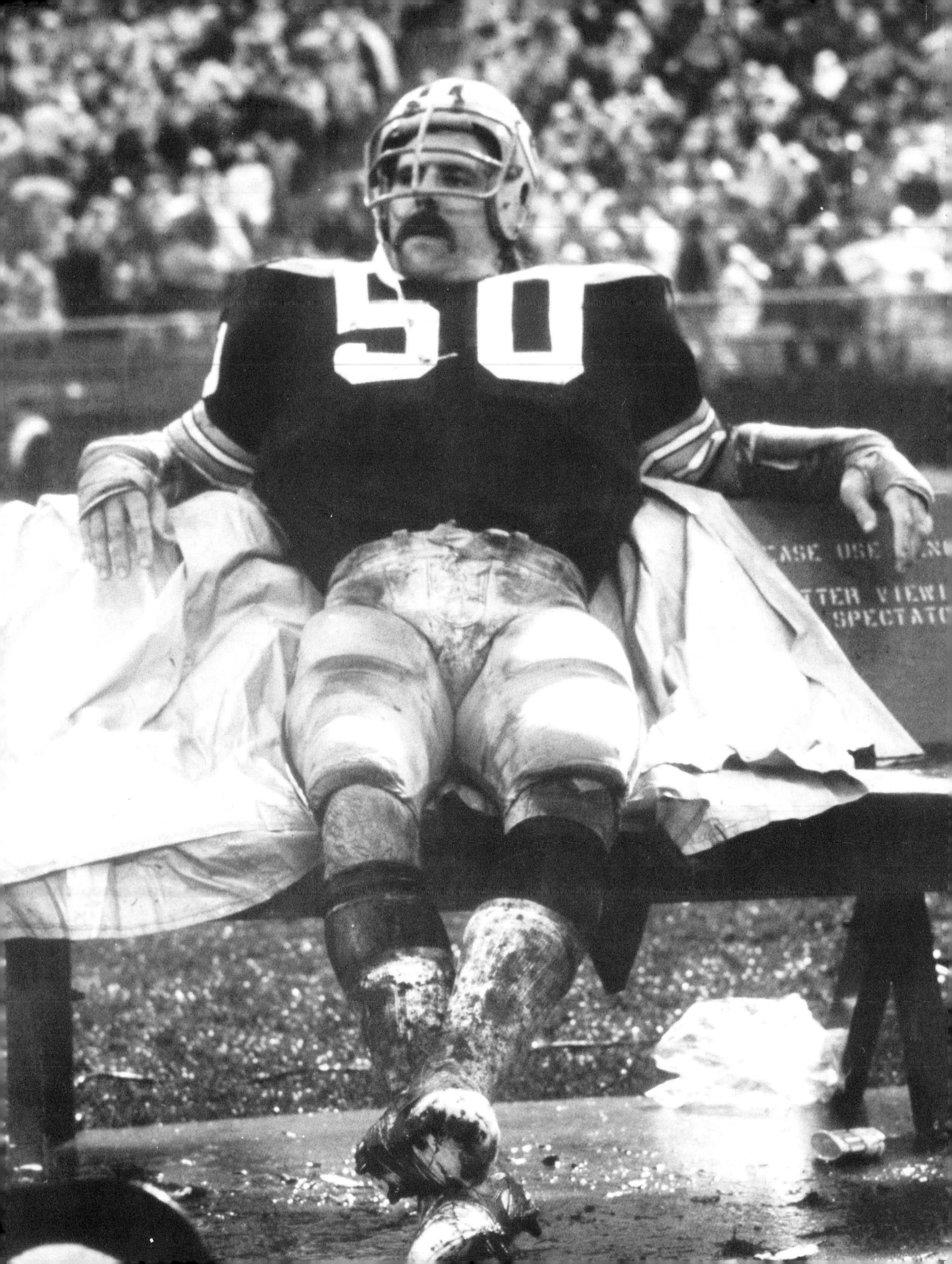

GO PACKERS GO
PACKER BACKERS
FROM
IRON RIVER, MICH.

28
GREEN BAY
AMERICA CITY
GO!! PACKERS
RAH/RAH! GREEN BAY PACKERS!

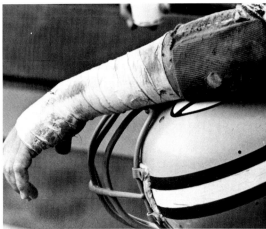

GREEN BAY PACKERS

The Green Bay Packers, an institution and a legend, are unique.

The only publicly-owned club in professional sport, they were founded as a town team in 1919 by E.L. "Curly" Lambeau, who coached them to six world championships. They acquired their first jerseys by persuading a packing company to put up money for equipment and, originally, played their games in an open field, where fans "passed the hat."

Nurtured into a professional football power that has left a lasting imprint on the sport, they became the first team to win three consecutive National Football League titles (1929-30-31), a feat repeated under Vince Lombardi (1965-66-67) and never equaled. Overall, they have won 11 world championships, more than any other club in league history.

Long a "state" team, annually playing games in Milwaukee as well as Green Bay, the Packers have become a national institution, with fans in all 50 states.

Erected 1977

Any man's finest hour—his greatest fulfillment to all he holds dear—is that moment when he has worked his heart out in a good cause and lies exhausted on the field of battle—VICTORIOUS

LEAVE NO REGRETS ON THE FIELD

73

Chapter 1

Titletown ... Still

"The closest thing to royalty that you could find anywhere in this country is the coach of the Green Bay Packers."

— Larry McCarren

Quite simply: It is the most unique, most special place on the American sports landscape.

The differences between Green Bay and anywhere else in the NFL seem staggering. And they're real. This sort of thing — a smallish, working man's town at the mouth of Wisconsin's Fox River competing for pro football supremacy with the New Yorks and Chicagos, all in the constant glare of national attention — just shouldn't be happening.

Logic cries out that the Packers ought to be extinct, like the Canton Bulldogs or the Pottstown Firebirds. And more times than anyone likes to count, they darn near were. The Green Bay franchise once was kept afloat because a man sold his car. It has gone into receivership, almost been sued out of business when an insurance company failed, nearly drifted away in the 1950s for lack of a modern stadium.

And yet, this phenomenon remains — as fascinating as ever, keeper of more pro football championships than any other city, once and still a legend.

"When you look at the Packers, it sometimes seems more like fiction than reality," current club president Bob Harlan said. "The history of this team is soap-opera stuff — except that nobody would write a script so unbelievable."

Everyone knows, of course, that the Packers are the only team in pro sports owned — strictly on a non-profit basis — by local shareholders. There were

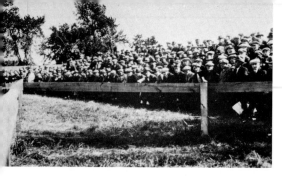

almost 1,900 at last count, area people and others who will never earn a dime from their investment. It says so right on their stock certificates, a stipulation that hasn't changed since 1923.

No matter.

In Green Bay, the Packers are family and always have been. The outfit Curly Lambeau patched together as a "town team" in 1919 may have become a multi-million dollar organization known nationwide, but it's still a down-home operation to the locals and throughout Wisconsin.

"There can't be anything else like this place," guard Rich Moran said after finishing his eighth year with the Pack in 1992. "I'm from the San Diego area, and out there everyone thought it was crazy when the Chargers made the playoffs. The fans were excited, the city was fired up.

"I had to laugh, because we have that sort of atmosphere in Green Bay just for training camp."

Coach Mike Holmgren put the Green Bay experience into a different perspective when he was hired off the staff of the San Francisco 49ers. Now remember, the 49ers won four Super Bowls in the 1980s, so it isn't exactly as though they were operating in isolation.

"Sure, I thought about the consequences of coming to a town where the football team was so important, where you'd be so much in the spotlight and everyone gets so personally involved," Holmgren said. "I thought about it but, as a coach, you're so busy and wrapped up in your work, I guess I thought the surroundings wouldn't have much impact.

"I knew it would be different from the Bay Area, obviously, but I had no idea *how* different.

"One story I've told a few places around the state sums it up. I was in a grocery store right after I took the job in Green Bay and I'm pushing a cart down this aisle. Well, there's an older lady coming the other way with her cart, and we're sort of approaching each other and I can tell she's looking at me with this funny expression.

"Finally, we get close to each other and she says, 'Hey, California, go out and kick some butt.' I was amazed, not only that she said what she did but that she knew I'd come from California and everything. I thought: These people are into it."

Holmgren is used to the fishbowl now. He's regularly stopped for football conversation by everyone from retirees to kids on the playground at his daughter's school. They all have something to say about the Packers and they all seem to know what they're talking about.

"Outsiders just can't believe how knowledgeable these fans are," said Gary Knafelc, a tight end during the Lombardi championship era and now public address announcer at Lambeau Field. "They're not just out there yelling and booing like people in other cities. They know what's going on, and you can't fool 'em."

They never tire of discussing the Pack, either.

"If you asked the average person on the street around here whether, if he were at a special dinner, he'd rather sit next to the President or a movie star or the coach of the Packers, the guy would definitely pick the coach," said Larry McCarren, who played center for the Pack from 1973–84 and stayed on in Green Bay as a TV broadcaster. "Everybody here wants to talk football, all the time."

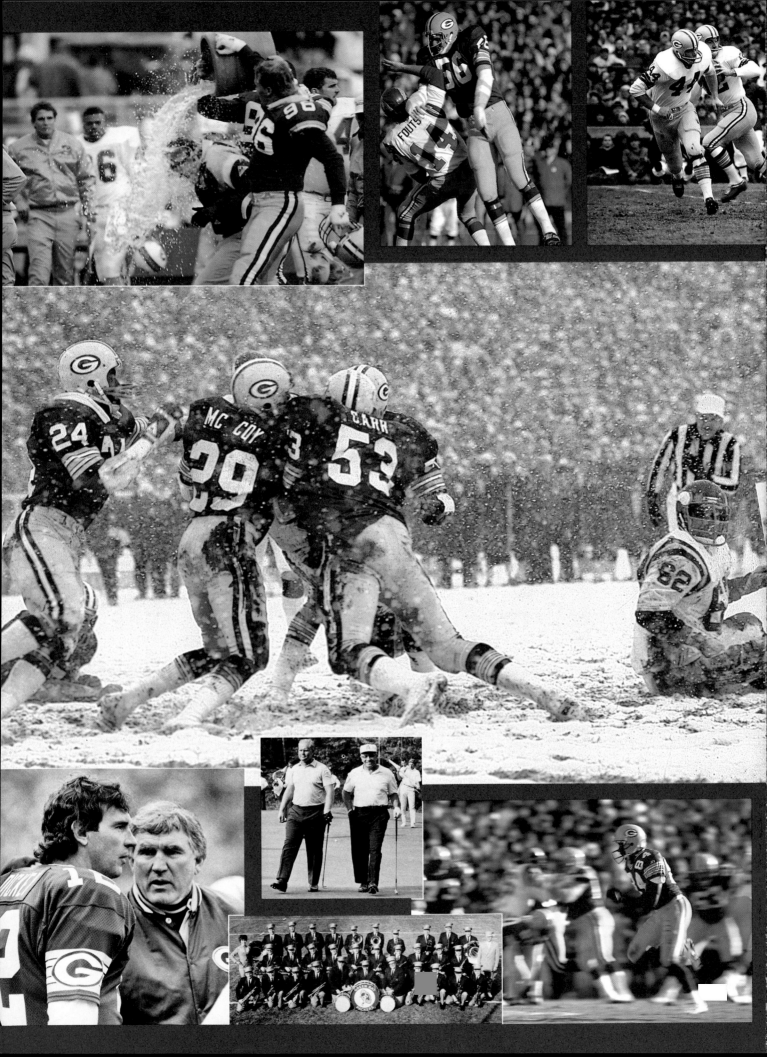

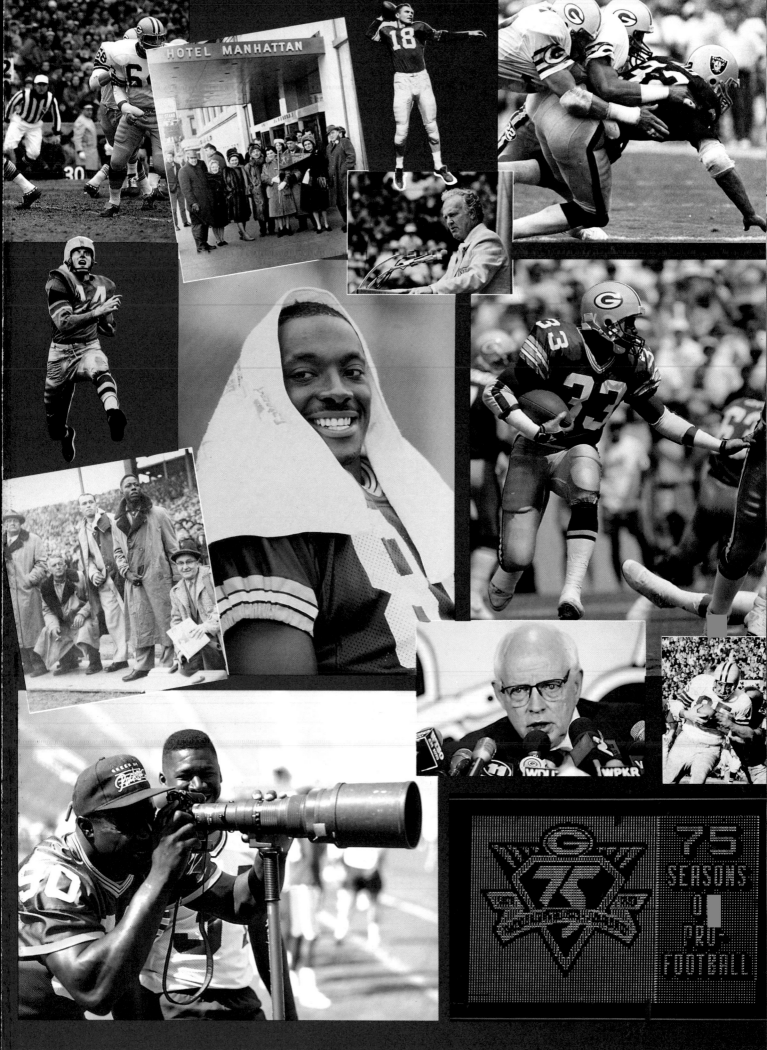

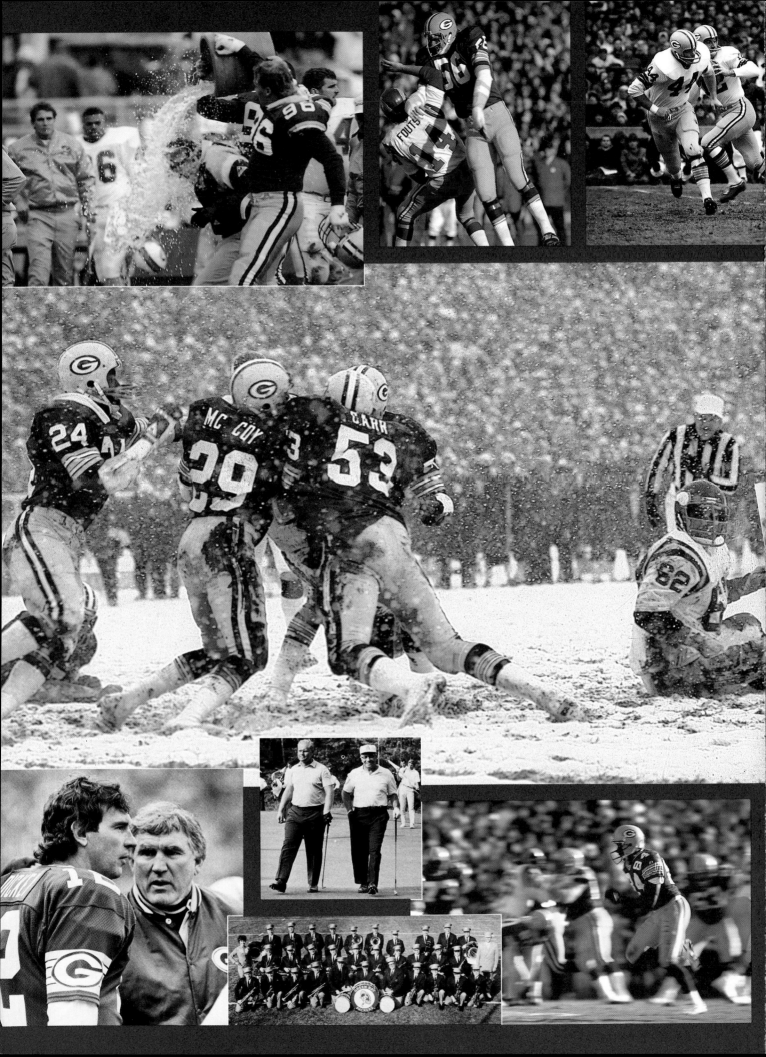

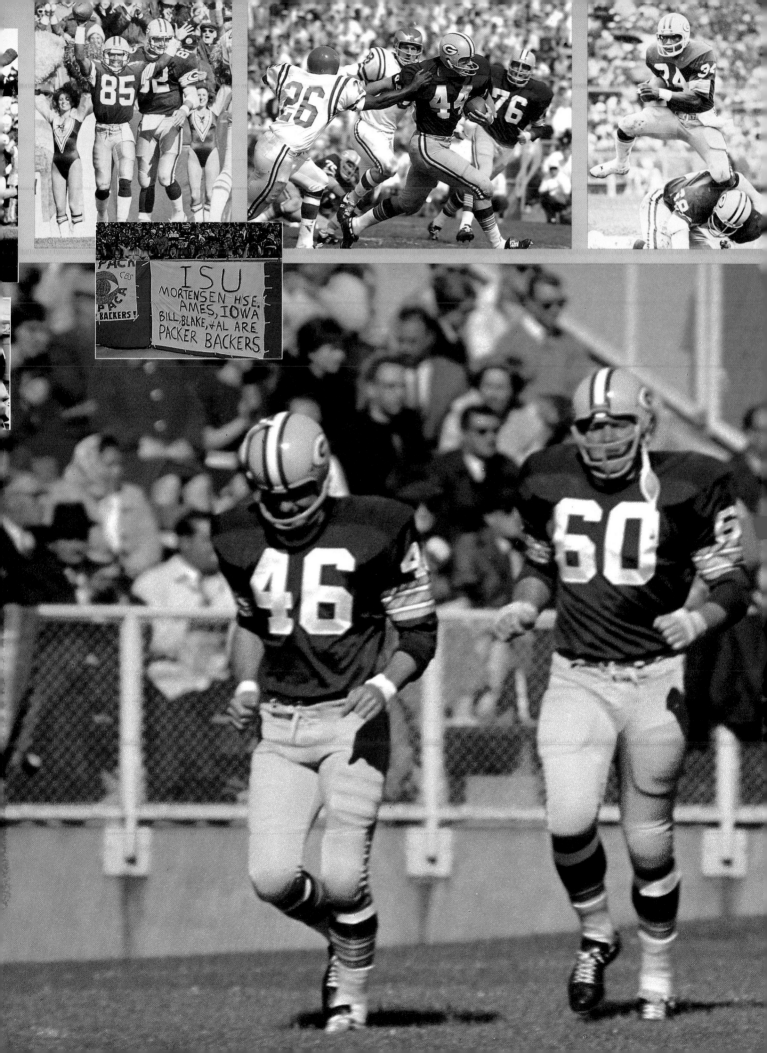

ISU
MORTENSEN H'SE.
AMES, IOWA
BILL, BLAKE, ¢AL ARE
PACKER BACKERS

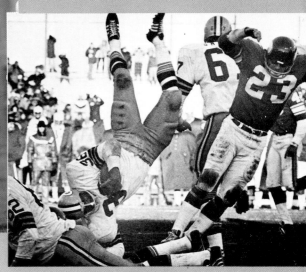

FRESH FROZEN FISH
FROM THE REAL REFRIGERATOR...
LAMBEAU FIELD!

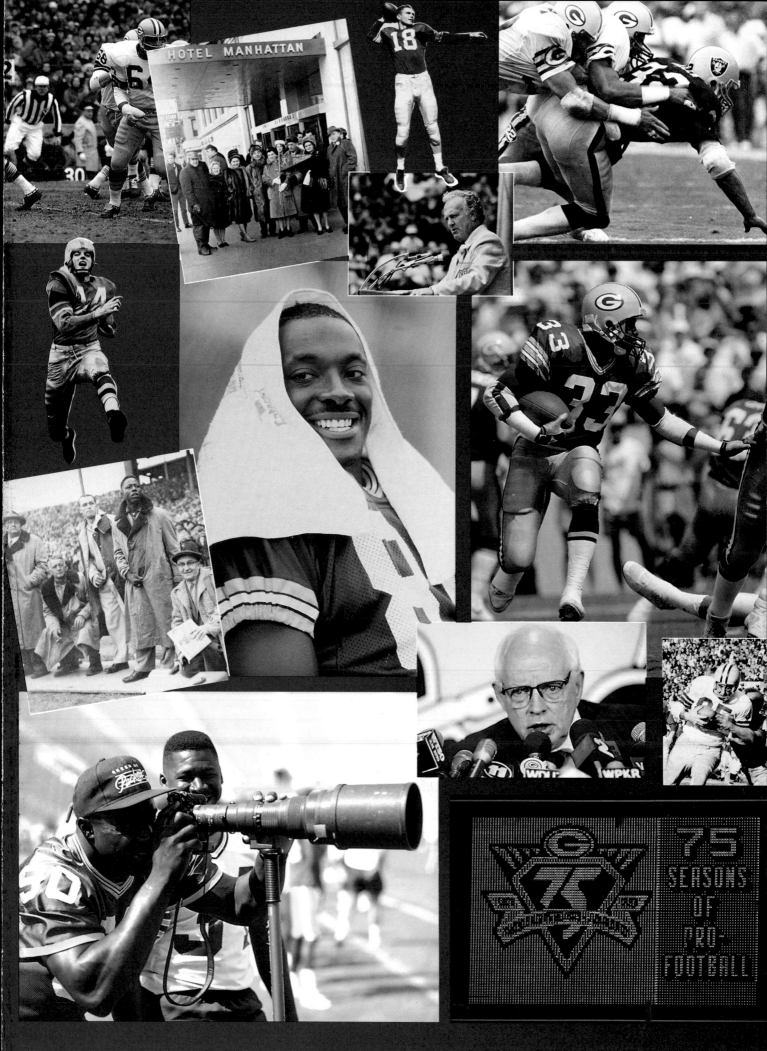

75 SEASONS OF PRO-FOOTBALL

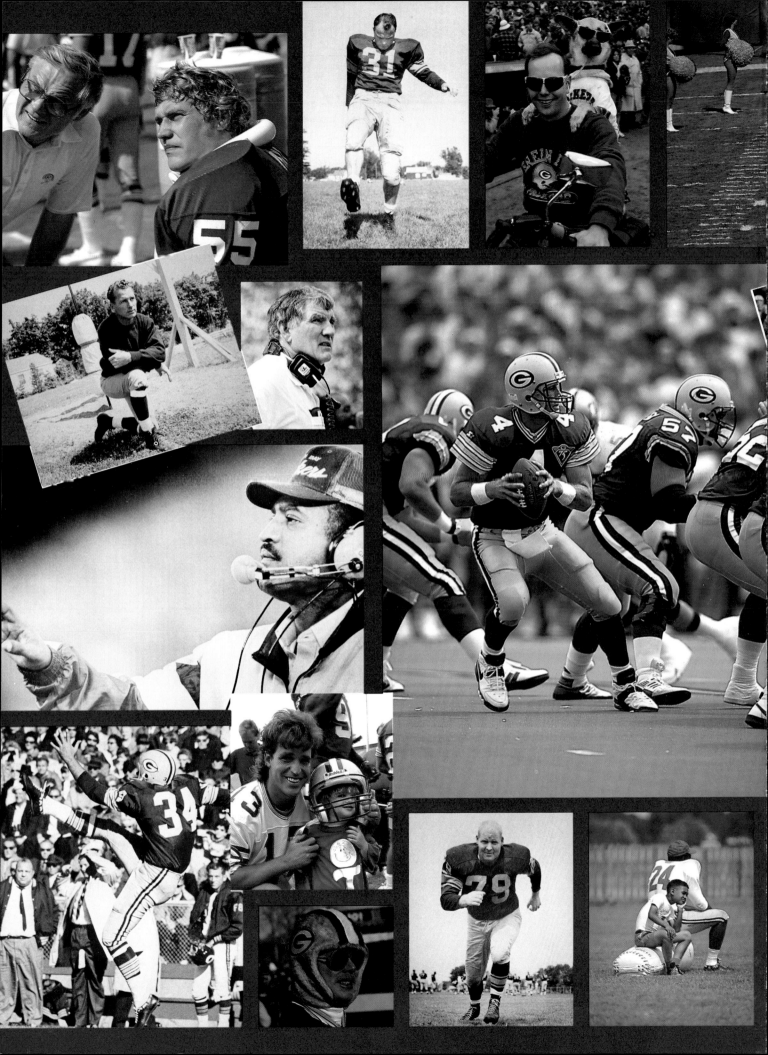

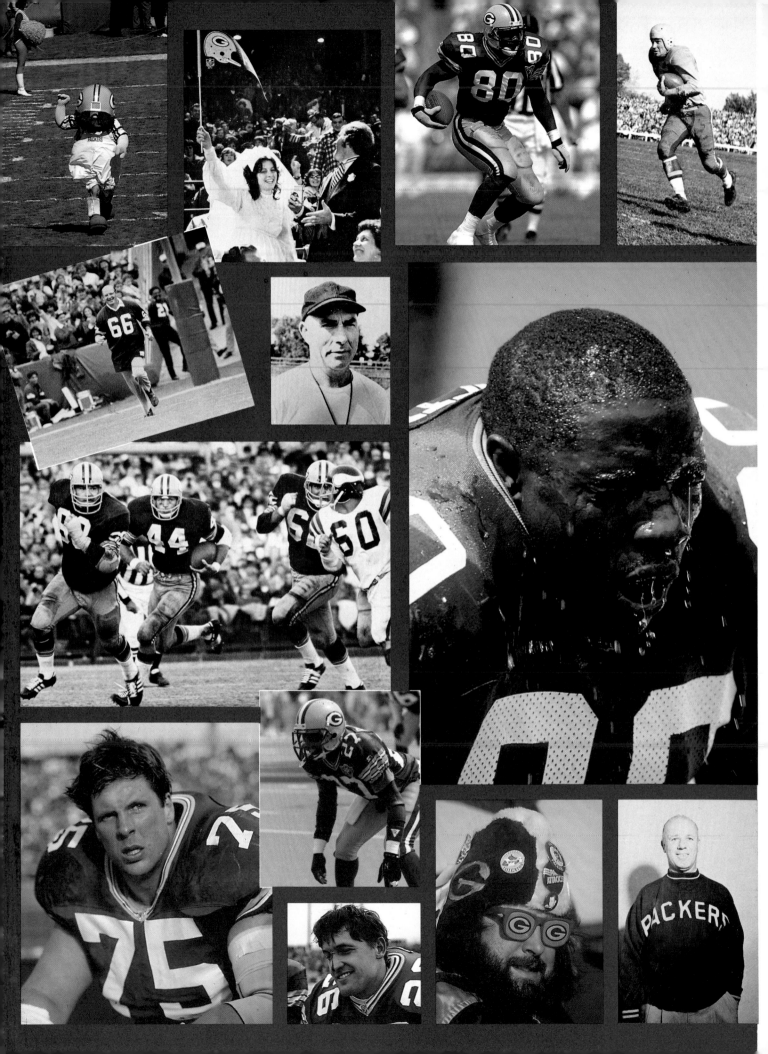

PACKER FANS

GO PACK GO

SONY

JumboTron

LAMBEAU FIELD-HOME OF

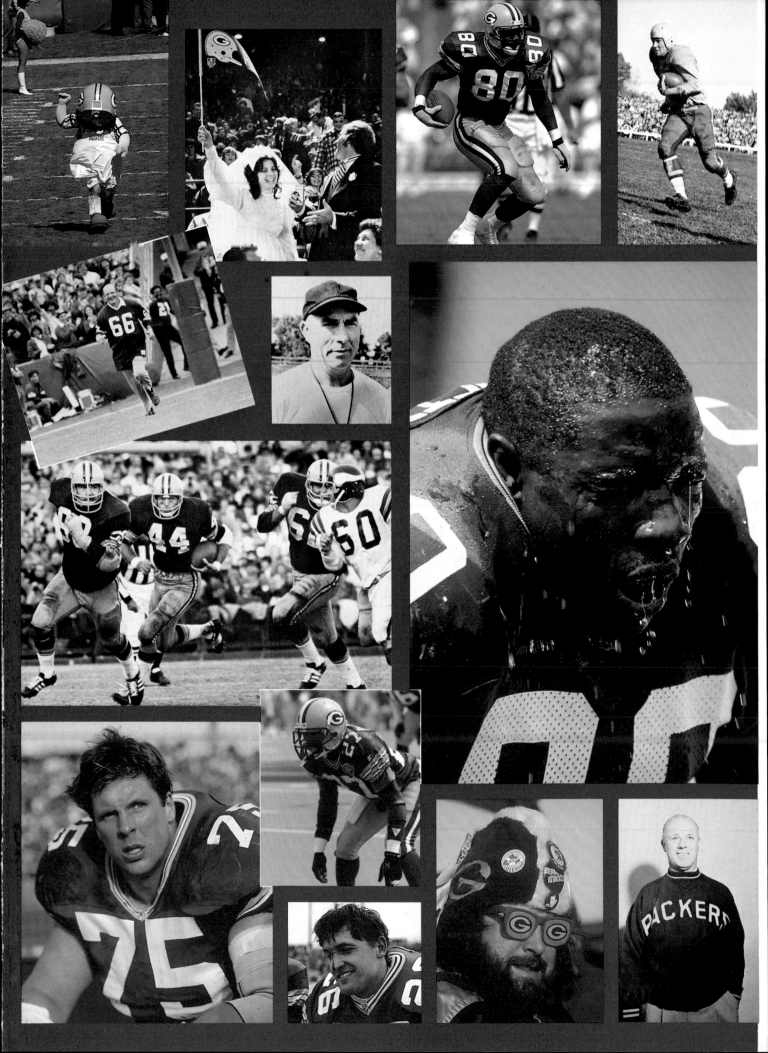

Current and former Packers mostly agree on something else, too; namely, that despite what the revered Lombardi said so often, winning isn't quite everything. They're not thrilled with so-so seasons, naturally, but the loyalists in Green Bay are happy with honest effort, with all-out football — whatever the result.

"This is a hard-working town with everyday people who represent a lot of old-fashioned ideas — good old ideas," said Tony Canadeo, a Hall of Fame running back who starred for the Packers in the 1940s, then stayed on as a broadcaster and eventually became a member of the team's executive committee and vice president of the organization. "These people don't want to hear fast-talking, quick-fix guys or see a team that won't hit and play hard.

"They'd like a team to work like they do and get along in the city. If a team does that, they'll return the loyalty over and over. They'll always forgive if it's about losing a game, but they don't care much for quitting."

Again, the comparison that comes to mind is that of family. Parents naturally hope their children will be academic whizzes and grow up to become wealthy, influential pillars of the community. But a lot of people don't reach such lofty station, and around Green Bay, folks apparently understand that trying as hard as you can is good enough.

One issue is beyond dispute: Interest in the Packers remains intense, through good times and bad.

It's been more than 20 years since the Pack won so much as a division

81

championship. The last of its 11 world titles came way back in 1967. In the years since Lombardi stepped aside after that '67 season, the Packers have done a lot more wrong than right. And not just on the field, either. There were some notorious cases of players' behavior becoming socially unacceptable and beyond — even breaking the law.

In the mid-1980s, defensive back Mossy Cade and popular, All-Pro wide receiver James Lofton each was arrested on sexual assault charges. In blue-collar Green Bay, where a shot and a beer after work doesn't exactly make you kin to the devil, fans pretty much had learned to tolerate a boys-will-be-boys approach from their football heroes. But the Cade-Lofton cases were so far beyond what was acceptable, the citizenry was dealt a couple of painful body blows.

Before the area could recover from those incidents, *Sports Illustrated* published a fairly damning article which portrayed Green Bay as a wasteland inhospitable to black athletes, too small to compete in the megabucks NFL, basically a relic from another age that now seemed almost irrelevant in a glitz-and-glamour sport.

It has turned out, obviously, that *Sports Illustrated*'s entire premise was about as worthless as packing your golf clubs to Wisconsin in January.

"With all the movement of free-agent players this past year, I must have taken 10 or 15 guys out to lunch who were in town for a visit," said Brett Favre, the Pack's wonderchild quarterback for the '90s. "Man, they all kept telling me how much they'd love to play in Green Bay and how they hoped it would work out. I've talked to guys around the whole league, too, and believe me, we don't have enough room to fit in all the guys who want to play here.

"This is the truth: There are 28 starting quarterbacks in the NFL, and I really think the other 27 all wish they had my job. Why wouldn't anybody want to play football in Green Bay?"

Favre's enthusiasm — and his assessment — have been reinforced by the number of big-name free agents who've signed with the Packers in the past year or two.

But if you go back a few seasons to a time when coaches were in

trouble, draft choices failed to pan out and the future wasn't as rosy, that magazine indictment was painful. What was worse, the Packers by that time had sunk to a level of consistent mediocrity — and sometimes below that. So the populace has had opportunities to grumble, to throw up its hands, to become bored or worse. In short, people could have gotten down on the Packers.

It didn't happen. Not in Green Bay.

Lambeau Field has been enlarged several times to accommodate demand, and the waiting list for season tickets remains so long that prospective buyers are told they might not make the blessed lists for 25 years or more.

Fr. Mike Weber, a priest who had worked with the Packers' equipment staff since 1961, offers a nice analogy.

"In that movie, *Field of Dreams,* there's a famous line: 'Build it and we will come,'" Weber said. "In Green Bay, they'll come whether you build anything or not."

When the Packers decided to add luxury boxes at Lambeau for the 1985 season, the announcement was made one weekday morning and, by noontime, the 24 proposed boxes all had been sold.

"People were phoning us that afternoon and complaining that we didn't notify them, that they didn't have a chance at a luxury box," Harlan said. "And really, even knowing what we know about Green Bay, that response was kind of a surprise. It seems funny now, but when we had our original discussions about the boxes, we wondered how they'd go over in a town like this.

"We sure found out. We added 44 more on the other side of the stadium, so for the start of the '85 season we had 68 boxes instead of the 24 we'd planned, and now there's a waiting list for those, too."

Actually, that kind of support — putting your money where your heart is — has existed from the start in Green Bay. The city literally has rescued the franchise several times.

These weren't just false crises, either. That business with the insurance company occurred in 1934, in the depths of the Depression, long before TV revenue and other big bucks came flowing into pro football.

What happened was that a set of bleachers at old City Stadium — adjacent to East High, where the Packers spent most of their years until the new stadium was built in 1957 — collapsed and a spectator was injured. He sued the team for $5,000, which was a lot of money at the time and certainly more than the financially strapped franchise had on hand. The problem was compounded when the Packers' insurance company went bankrupt and other losses had to be covered, as well.

The team was forced into receivership, and really, it only stayed afloat because longtime supporter and former club president Lee Joannes put up $6,000 of his own money. There were lean, worrying years ahead, but eventually — in part because superstar Don Hutson came along in 1935 and also because local citizens purchased more stock — the corporation became solvent again in 1937.

Another fiscal thunderhead arose in 1949, at the end of Lambeau's incredible tenure as the Packers' major domo. Lambeau had made a serious error purchasing Rockwood Lodge, a famous local structure, to serve as team headquarters. He went through plenty of the corporation's money decorating the place, as well, which turned into an utter waste — in part because the ground around the lodge was unsuitable for football and the whole grand notion of using it as a practice facility had to be scrapped.

The Packers were desperately short of cash again, so on Thanksgiving Day in '49, the team staged what amounted to an intrasquad scrimmage — along with cameo appearances from onetime heroes like Hutson and quarterback Arnie Herber — as a fund-raiser. It snowed buckets that Thanksgiving, but enough fans turned up that the team pocketed $50,000 just when potential bankruptcy was hovering around the corner.

It didn't hurt that Rockwood Lodge burned to the ground the following year — handing the team a $75,000 insurance windfall — but the bottom line was that the people of Green Bay once again had rallied to keep their football team at a time when all the other small-town franchises had long since given up the ghost.

Then there's the matter of Lambeau Field itself.

The NFL was coming into its own in the 1950s, with television on the horizon and fans flocking to see the game's stars in America's giant cities. And there sat the Packers, with City Stadium pretty much falling down around them.

It was obvious that Green Bay needed a new structure, with additional seating and suitable amenities, just to remain in the league.

After studies had been completed and a site picked out, citizens were asked to reach into their wallets again. The stadium, which would be the

joint responsibility of the city and the Packers, could only be built with money raised through a bond issue. It's important to note that, for all their previous heroics and six NFL titles, the Packers had gone a decade without a winning season and were playing fairly uninspiring football when the referendum came to a vote.

One thing that helped was that the actual amount needed was only $969,000, which would buy a lot of spaghetti dinners but nonetheless is an outright trifle compared to the cost of other, less well-appointed stadiums. The cost was kept down — and here's this theme again — because the city's public works department agreed to handle water and sewer service and paving the parking lots. Likewise, Brown County's highway department took on the ground-moving phase of construction at bare-bones cost.

Need proof what the Packers and their rich history meant to the NFL? Old friend and rival George Halas of the Chicago Bears actually came to Green Bay for a huge rally supporting the stadium vote.

And so the bond issue passed, by a remarkable 2–1 margin. The townspeople had saved their Packers once more.

"When you think about it, a lot of small towns had pro football teams at one time or another," Hall of Fame quarterback Bart Starr said. "They've all died, all but the Packers. Green Bay survived because of its people — through their dedication, loyalty, hard work and support.

"Sure, there was some good fortune involved. Coach Lombardi came

One thing about Packer fans: They're always willing to help officials make the proper call, just as they did in a 1960s game when Baltimore's Bobby Boyd got a little too eager while trying to break up a pass intended for Bob Long. Everyone watches intently as the ball arrived, but suddenly there are thousands of helpers trying to throw a penalty flag when Boyd commits pass interference.

along just at the right time and we won championships. Television brought football into another era and provided a lot of money for a team that sometimes had struggled financially.

"But if the people of Green Bay hadn't stuck with it long after all those other small-town teams disappeared, none of the good fortune ever could have happened. There's no way to describe it except to say that these people are just absolutely sensational."

And as Starr noted, they've all shared in creating something no one else has.

"You can't really compare the Packers to any other franchise," he said. "They're totally unique, one of a kind. The success of the Green Bay Packers is now something global."

Besides the obvious financial and emotional support, there is another intriguing aspect to the relationship between the Packers and their fans. Both sides seem to know instinctively that it's a two-way affair.

For instance, there's the issue of patience. Green Bay hung in there with its heroes during the down years between Lambeau and Lombardi. The reward was five more championships in a run of success that may never be challenged — anytime, anywhere.

There's been a similar resolve during the post-Lombardi struggles. Perhaps it's because the town has such an enduring population base — people tend to stay on through generations — but Green Bay fans have shown dogged patience. And with it, this remarkable kind of resolve that says, yes, it may take awhile but eventually another dynasty is coming.

"Even though they've been disappointed a lot of times and through a lot of changes, people here somehow retain that championship feeling," Holmgren said. "It's like nothing ever went away.

"Sometimes you think that 25 years since they won never happened, like it's been locked in a vault. Like Bart Starr and the Super Bowls and everything was just a couple of years ago. It's amazing."

So it is.

Former running back Travis Williams, who played just four seasons (1967–70) with the Packers, died in 1991. Yes, Williams had a spectacular

rookie season when he set an NFL record for kickoff returns and the Packers won their second Super Bowl, but he faded relatively quickly from the scene.

Still, when news of Williams' passing reached town two decades after his last game for the Pack, a huge floral arrangement was delivered to Lambeau Field and placed in the end zone. A large card alongside the flowers contained a message to the effect that Travis would always be loved and remembered.

In another vein altogether, ponder this parcel of proof that, when it comes to football, yesterday and tomorrow blend together in this part of the country: A visitor to Green Bay in 1993 could flip the dial on his car radio and hear this particular slogan: "WJLW — Titletown's only continuous FM country music!"

Titletown?

Lyndon Johnson was president the last time Green Bay won a title, but the image endures. You can sleep over in the Titletown Motel or, in case you're moving to town, go shopping for a house with Titletown Realty.

"I meet people all the time who can talk about the Ice Bowl like it was last year," Favre said. "They'll remember who sat where and what they thought. Not just that game, either. People will come up and say, 'The way you drop back reminds me of so-and-so in such-and-such a year.' It's incredible. Most people in other places can't remember what happened last week."

Maybe the rest of America thought the Packers just disappeared with the end of the Lombardi era, but in Wisconsin, they'll beg to differ.

Perhaps people elsewhere were shocked when the Packers won the much-publicized battle for free-agent superstar Reggie White. In Green Bay, though, the reaction was excitement but not necessarily surprise. Packer fans still routinely assume that if it was good enough for Starr and Hutson and Ray Nitschke and Forrest Gregg, this place ought to be just fine for somebody like Reggie White.

After all, when Reggie's almost-certain induction day arrives, he'll merely become the 23rd Packer in the pro football Hall of Fame. At least the 23rd, since several other Green Bay superstars remain on the waiting list at Canton.

"Anyone who knows football history realizes what the Green Bay Packers mean to our game," said Ron Wolf, the general manager charged with initiating the franchise's next golden era. "This is hallowed ground.

"So many great players and coaches have walked these halls, it's overwhelming. Here's how I choose to think of the Packers: In our sport, there's a game at the end of the year to determine the champion. It's called the Super Bowl, and the winner receives a trophy which represents excellence — a symbol of excellence.

"It's called the Lombardi Trophy, and in football, Coach Lombardi represented excellence and the Packers represented excellence.

"And believe me when I tell you that the people of Green Bay know their football history." ❖

Chapter 2

Saint Vincent

"Football must be a game for madmen, and I must be one of them."

— Vince Lombardi

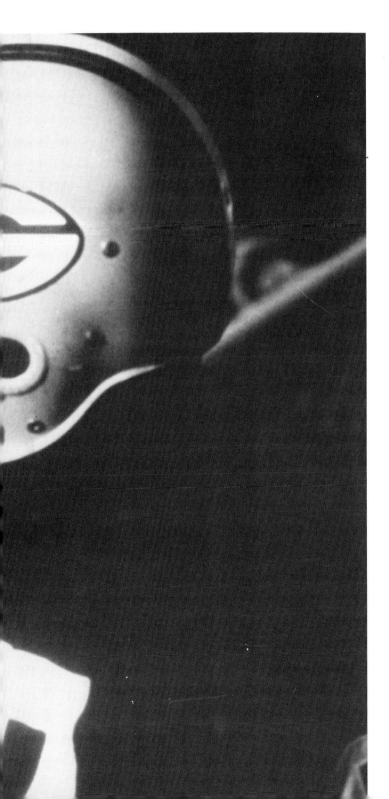

Saint or madman?

Vincent Thomas Lombardi was neither — though at times he was called both, sometimes moments apart. He also has been described as committed, abrasive, loyal, driven, loving, a maniac, a teacher, a role model, a pussycat, a beast. Not to mention stubborn, emotional, egotistical, generous, brilliant, passionate and larger than life.

Incredible as it seems, a case can be made that Lombardi fit every one of those adjectives, nouns and more — sometimes simultaneously, as impossible as that sounds when you consider so many apparently contradictory traits.

But then again, Lombardi also was straightforward and yet complex, all at once.

The only thing about him that remains simple to digest 35 years after his arrival in Wisconsin and more than two decades following his death is the record: Lombardi's Packers went 98–30–4 from 1959–67 and won five NFL championships in one magnificent seven-year stretch — including three in a row in the coach's final three seasons.

Nobody ever had won three straight under the league's two-division format — Green Bay did it under legendary founder Curly Lambeau in 1929–31 — and Lombardi constantly hammered at his athletes during the grueling '67 season that the feat might never be accomplished again.

And so far it hasn't.

Lombardi could be jovial and forthcoming with the media, or downright difficult. But he was obviously getting on well with *Press-Gazette* reporter Lee Remmel in this interview — perhaps suspecting that Remmel eventually would join the club as its public relations director.

He was big news before his Packers even played a game. Reporters flocked out to greet Lombardi and his wife, Marie, when they arrived in Green Bay for the big move from New York. Long-time Packer President Dominic Olejniczak (right) extended an official welcome.

"I want it," he shouted over and over at a proud but aging and banged-up team. "I deserve it. You deserve it."

Lombardi's last two teams also made history by winning Super Bowls I and II. Just four games were played between the NFL champion and the American Football League winner before an eventual merger in 1970, and the Packers were the only team from the established league to uphold tradition. Baltimore and Minnesota were upset back to back in Super Bowls III and IV, and former Packers still smile at the notion that Coach Lombardi never would have permitted such a thing.

"There is simply no way that he was going to let us lose that football game," offensive tackle and co-captain Bob Skoronski said of the much-hyped Super Bowl I. "He made up his mind it just would not happen."

And it didn't. The Packers stormed back from a shaky first half to swamp Kansas City 35–10.

So that's the Lombardi record, and yes, it's stunning.

A career assistant coach, he took over the Packers after they'd gone 1–10–1 in 1958 under Scooter McLean, who everyone around the team thought squandered some talent because he was just too nice a guy. That season was such a disaster that Green Bay native Red Smith, who went on to win the Pulitzer Prize as a *New York Times* columnist, was moved to write: "The Packers overwhelmed one opponent, underwhelmed 10 and whelmed one."

Lombardi burst onto the scene in '59 — plucked from the New York Giants, where he'd been offensive coordinator — and changed the face of Green Bay football. The Packers shocked the rival Chicago Bears in their opener, eventually finished 7–5 that season, Lombardi got a $10,000 bonus from a grateful executive board and things were never the same again.

A dynasty was born.

Also a legend.

Oh, and there was never any danger this Lombardi fellow might fail because he was too nice. At least not on the football field.

As remarkable as it is, Lombardi's record of seemingly endless dramatic victories and occasional, landmark defeats barely gets the story started. Sure, he was a winner of epic proportions — hey, Green Bay renamed a street after him while he was still alive — but so many other things about Lombardi combined to make him one of the most important, most charismatic people in football history.

"Part of it was the man himself," said quarterback Bart Starr, who became a Hall of Famer under Lombardi. "Never mind his disposition — a big deal has always been made about the yelling and screaming. He was actually a role model because he not only won, but he did it without ever changing his priorities.

"There was never a compromise, not in how he approached things or how the team did. Coach used to say we should consider God first, our family second and the Green Bay Packers third. Sometimes we'd kid among ourselves that he'd mix up that order once in awhile, but it was just that: joking.

"Coach Lombardi stayed true to what he believed in, and he was capable of making others believe in it, too. Being able to play for him was the greatest thing that ever happened to me as an athlete."

Starr makes another point about Lombardi's ultimate place in the game.

"Besides his approach and the type of person he was, and also the success he had, you have to remember that our teams of that time came along just as television was bringing pro football into the limelight," he said.

"So Lombardi's era coincided with a huge boom in the NFL's popularity. That helped make him the legend he became, but it also worked the other way. His mystique and the Packers' great success helped build the game's image, as well."

There's certainly no question about the huge shadow Lombardi cast on football in general and Green Bay in particular. Or how it lingers.

So many books have been written about this man — including a couple he did himself — that it might be easier to look up the boyhood accomplishments of Vince Lombardi than research the early days of Alexander the Great. Lombardi has been featured in magazine profiles, motivational films and TV specials. Toward the end of his life, he became one of the most moving public speakers in or out of sports.

Every Packer who played on the 1959 team recalls Lombardi's first team gathering as though it happened a week ago. Most discuss that introduction the way you'd expect converts to talk about a spiritual revelation.

"I get chills just thinking about it," guard Fuzzy Thurston said. "You knew from the moment he walked in the room that something great was going to happen. There's almost no way to describe it."

Starr says he was so excited hearing Lombardi address the team for the first time that he bolted out at the end of the meeting, ran to a pay phone and called home.

"Honey, we're going to start winning again," Starr told his wife, Cherry.

And that was after one talk.

"When Lombardi walked in any room, he just took over," Thurston said. "There's a lot of conversation these days about being focused. That's the big phrase. Well, nobody knows what focused really is unless they saw Lombardi."

Thurston's running mate at guard, Jerry Kramer, wrote several popular books and has become something of an insider-historian concerning the Lombardi-era Packers.

Kramer always gets around to one story about an evening early in the Packers' 1959 training camp at St. Norbert's College — when Lombardi arrived for a routine bed-check. Kramer was rooming with fullback Jim Taylor.

"At 11 on the dot one night, Vince came by our room," Kramer said, "and Jimmy was sitting on the edge of his bed with his socks and shorts on.

"Coach said, 'Jimmy, what time you got?'

"Jimmy whipped out his watch and said, 'I've got 11 o'clock, sir.'

"'Jimmy, you're supposed to be in bed at 11, aren't you?' Coach said.

"'Yes, sir,' said Jimmy.

"Coach said, 'Jimmy, that'll cost you $25.'

"Jimmy looked at me open-mouthed and I raised my eyebrows a little bit and said, 'Oooh, this guy's pretty serious.'"

And of course, it'd be hard to find a fan who hasn't chuckled over a few of Lombardi's infamous exchanges with free-spirited wide receiver Max McGee.

Like the time Lombardi seemed ready to explode because, even as he increased fines for unexcused late-night departures, McGee had broken curfew yet again. Max had been docked $50, then $100. And then $500. By which time Lombardi's Italian temper was off the Richter scale.

"If I catch you again, it'll be a thousand bucks!" Lombardi screeched. And then he smiled and said: "And Max, if there's something out there worth a thousand dollars, call me and I'll go with you."

Perhaps the best give-and-take with McGee, though, came during a team meeting when Lombardi was furious over what he considered the Packers' particularly sloppy play the previous Sunday.

"We're going to get back to fundamentals," the coach said sarcastically. Then picking up a prop, he added: "This is a football."

From the back of the room, McGee hollered, "Wait a minute, Coach. You're going too fast."

There are a million more Lombardi stories — many, many worth retelling — but the point here is that so many of these moments already have been documented and recalled that Lombardi remains a household name despite a relatively short head coaching career and the fact that he died of cancer in 1970. If you don't know anything about Vince Lombardi — his moods, his singlemindedness, his relentless pursuit of excellence and his impact on the entire sport — then, sorry, you probably couldn't tell the difference between a football and badminton birdie.

If there's such a person in Green Bay, Brown County or even the state of Wisconsin, he's keeping it quiet or remaining well hidden.

Even casual fans remember all the pertinent details — that Lombardi was Brooklyn-born, played on a rugged line at Fordham that became known as the Seven Blocks of Granite, began his coaching career at St. Cecilia's High School in New Jersey, apprenticed with the legendary Earl Blaik at Army and learned the pro game during a tenure with the Giants.

And they know that, after his unparalleled run with the Packers, Lombardi relinquished all coaching duties and tried to stay on as general manager alone — while longtime assistant Phil Bengtson took over the toughest job in sports as his successor. And that, missing the sideline with a desperation he didn't know existed, Lombardi eventually moved on to Washington, where he whipped, prodded and urged a previously sickly Redskin team to a winning season in 1969.

Those are the facts, they're well known and they've been repeated so often that the particular, unique character of Vince Lombardi sometimes gets swamped by his resume. He was, very definitely, more than his won-lost record.

For one thing, Lombardi's glory years in Green Bay occurred in the 1960s, but he probably belonged to another time altogether. Maybe even to days of knights and kings, when honor and loyalty and crusades for the common welfare were a man's tests of goodness.

Ironically, Kramer hinted at that sort of connection after the Packers

drove 67 yards in the final minutes to beat Dallas 21–17 in the Ice Bowl —
that storied NFL title game of 1967 which was played on a frozen field
with everyone numbed by the howling wind and temperatures around
13 below.

Starr's quarterback sneak for the winning touchdown as the seconds
ticked away has become perhaps the most famous play in pro football
history, but that entire season was, yes, a crusade for Lombardi and his
team — the quest for a third consecutive championship.

They fought through injuries — to Starr, among others — and some
key changes in personnel. Hall of Fame running backs Taylor and Paul
Hornung were both gone by then. The Packers struggled with every
other kind of adversity and somehow got it done, like warriors from the
distant past rising up for a last great conquest.

How fitting that it should end, not just in victory, but with players
fighting frostbite and Lombardi defying all conventional strategy — kick
the field goal for a tie and overtime, or at least throw a pass to stop the
clock for another play.

"There's so much love on this team," Kramer told wide-eyed reporters
after the game. "Perhaps we're living in Camelot."

Lombardi's analysis of the game's last few ticks belonged to another
time, too.

Though he endorsed the change and believed it was best for everyone involved at the time, Lombardi clearly was moved at the press conference announcing that longtime assistant Phil Bengtson would become head coach for the 1968 season.

"If you can't run the ball and gain one foot," he thundered, "you don't deserve to win the game."

It wouldn't have been right, and Lombardi insisted that things be done right. Not just correctly, or efficiently, but right.

For instance, he never would have allowed dirty football. He wouldn't have played it loose and jiggled with the rules. He demanded victory, but only if it could be fair and square. And despite what cynics believed, he slept soundly after a loss if he felt in his heart that his team had given its best.

A couple of incidents attest to Lombardi's fierce adherence to principle. They occurred just a few weeks apart near the end of that record-setting '67 season.

The first came on the next-to-last date of the regular season. The Packers had clinched their division and could have waltzed through the final two games, resting for a brutal playoff run. But they had an assignment in Los Angeles, where the Rams were fighting for their own division title against Baltimore.

The natural tendency would have been for Green Bay to come out flat, perhaps presenting the Rams with a critical victory without much fuss.

Lombardi knew what people would say if Los Angeles won easily, so he drove his tired team unmercifully during preparations that week. He made it clear he expected to win — whether it meant a damn thing in the standings or not.

"We are the Green Bay Packers and we are a proud football team," he said.

As it happened, the Rams won anyway — on a blocked punt, after a wild, furiously contested war that Lombardi later said he wanted desperately. Angry as he might have been at losing, Lombardi conceded he was, indeed, proud of the Packers for their effort and intensity.

Los Angeles Times columnist Jim Murray wrote of that day: "It is a measure of the man that he went all out Saturday to win a game he would have been far better off losing. For, if he handed Baltimore a championship by winning Saturday, the Colts would have been given two weeks to prepare for him. They could have sent Johnny Unitas home to sit in a rocking chair and study his Green Bay playbook. They could have tiptoed through the Ram game and lost with a shrug.

"And yet, Lombardi's team went down with all guns firing, the flag still flying, looking for ways to clobber the Rams and stopping the clock to do it. The Rams came out of it looking like guys who had just broken up a dog fight.

"I don't care what your profession is, if you don't have any respect for it, you'll never be any good at it. I have seen great journalists, outwardly cynical toward their work, turn physically sick when they hear about a brother newsman on the take, or given to printing lies because he's too lazy or too lousy to look for the truth.

"There are large areas of the world where coaching football may equate in the common mind with watching a cannon in the park or polishing the statue of Sherman's horse.

"But to Vince Lombardi, it's his profession. He would quit before he would dishonor it. If there were only three people in the world who

Though he could be tough on them at practice, Lombardi loved his players and was happy to pose with some of his stars — (from left) Jim Ringo, Boyd Dowler, Ron Kramer, Bart Starr and Jim Taylor.

knew what it was or how difficult it was, it would still be a matter of pride to him to excel at it.

"... Vince Lombardi's face was suffused with pride. All he lost was a game. But he hadn't tried to sell the Green Bay Packers with one wheel missing or the engine failing. He hadn't come into town with a plastic team craftily disguised as the real thing. His team lived up to the warranty. No one wanted his money back. No one hollered for the Better Business Bureau.

"His critics have said Lombardi doesn't belong in this century. And they are right. Pride in workmanship like that hasn't been seen much in this century."

The Packers went on to defeat those very same Rams 28–7 in the first round of the playoffs at Milwaukee, and then came the Ice Bowl showdown with Dallas.

Believe it or not, despite all his exhilaration and excitement with that triumph, Lombardi fretted over one aspect of the game.

The turf at Lambeau Field had frozen solid, it turned out, because a heating system — which happened to be Lombardi's pet project — didn't work. The coach was distraught when he discovered what had

A rarity: The city of Green Bay changed the name of Highland Avenue to Lombardi Avenue after the coach resigned to concentrate on the general manager's job after the 1967 season.

happened, even though he knew the rock-hard surface might benefit the Packers far more than the warm-weather Cowboys.

"They'll think I did it on purpose," Lombardi wailed.

Not in a million years, but that was the kind of fair play the man demanded of himself and everyone else.

And while Lombardi sounded at times like a tyrant who refused to answer to anyone but himself, the truth is he never jumped above his proper place.

Former NFL commissioner Pete Rozelle recalled Lombardi telling him: "If you're going to demand respect for authority, you've got to give it."

And Lombardi was as good as his word.

"One thing that made him so unique is that he not only had the right priorities, but he stuck by them," Starr said. "He wouldn't turn his back on what he believed in the heat of battle.

"He didn't really teach us about football as much as he taught us about life. And in the process, we happened to become a very good, very confident football team. But he always stuck to the bigger picture, the more important values. That takes a very special person."

Center Bill Curry, who played two seasons during Lombardi's early years at Green Bay and then went on to win a Super Bowl with Baltimore, at first refused to believe the coach was sincere when he talked about loyalty and the team as a family.

Curry felt that, once a player left Green Bay, Lombardi would cast him aside. So naturally Curry was stunned years later when he bumped into Lombardi and was treated not only with warmth, but like a successful son who'd gone on to great things elsewhere.

The effect was more than a little dramatic.

So there was Curry, standing at Lombardi's bedside in 1970 as the coach lay dying.

"You meant a great deal to my life," Curry said.

"And you could mean a great deal to mine," Lombardi told him, "if you'll pray for me."

If Lombardi belonged in another era or another century in his personal beliefs, it's a temptation to think the same thing carried over to his football strategy.

Watching the Packers on television or reading opinions from the ill-informed, you'd have thought Lombardi knew nothing of Xs and Os, that he ranted on about blocking and tackling but only knew about five or six plays. At times it was suggested that Lombardi hungered in his heart for the days of the flying wedge, one-platoon football and no such thing as the forward pass.

And occasionally he issued very quotable statements wanting his teams to be physical, such as the time he said, "Dancing is a contact sport. Football is a collision sport."

True enough, he preached execution and he knew you couldn't win without running the ball and knocking people down. He would never countenance panty-waist football. Vince Lombardi wasn't a likely candidate to buy the run-and-shoot offense.

"We have to do what we do and do it well," Lombardi repeated again and again, referring in part to the now-famous Green Bay Sweep — the powerhouse play that made heroes of Taylor, Hornung and even those offensive linemen who pulled and led the running backs. The sweep became Lombardi's signature.

Likewise, he saw the battle at the line of scrimmage as a test of wills. If you couldn't win that, you couldn't win championships.

"Lombardi was almost a fanatic about goal-line offense," Thurston recalled. "We practiced it every day. He didn't believe we should ever be stopped down close to the goal line, because that was the area where your heart and your execution got the job done. He hated being stopped down close more than anything."

But right at this point in any retrospective, appearances can be deceiving.

Lombardi actually was a master tactician — albeit a guy who didn't want to make things any more complicated than necessary. Most of the Packers — Starr in particular — gave the coach almost total credit for their 34–27 victory over Dallas in the 1966 title game.

Lombardi had juggled the playbook, and more or less reversed all the Packers' formation tendencies. Plays that had come from one set throughout the season suddenly were being run out of another. The confused Cowboys played as though dizzied from watching a movie that was being run backwards.

The same kind of thing happened a year later in the playoff rematch against the Rams. Lombardi devised a scheme in which tight end Marv Fleming moved in to double-team All-Pro defensive end Deacon Jones, leader of the Fearsome Foursome that had terrorized so many passers.

Jones never got a sniff in the Packers' three-touchdown victory.

"Lombardi gave us so much confidence — both on offense and defense," Skoronski said. "We were always prepared. For every play, we had a counter. If one thing didn't work, there was a counter play that would.

"You always felt like he had the answer."

Most of the time, Lombardi's players felt as though he might have all the questions, too. He could be difficult, caustic, overbearing, almost cruel in his criticisms — though everyone agrees he never held a grudge and might put his arm around somebody for a friendly chat just minutes after a horrible tongue-lashing.

Even some players who found Lombardi's verbal abuse annoying are quick to admit that, whatever else you thought about the man, he was a magician at getting the most from whatever talent was available.

"You hear Jerry (Kramer) and some of the other guys talking about Lombardi and saying that he was kind of a father figure to them," center Ken Bowman said. "I wouldn't go that far, personally. I don't think I'd have wanted him to be my father.

"But I'll tell you, he was an incredible teacher. He found ways to make whatever point it was, to hold your attention, to get through and find the results he wanted. He definitely made players better."

And by all accounts, Lombardi loved 'em — whether they became all-pros like Hornung, his personal favorite, or just guys who worked hard at the game. The coach also was ahead of his time in another sense, since he was utterly blind to race or ethnic background.

Leaving the sidelines was a mistake, as Lombardi found out soon enough. During the 1968 season, he was a caged lion while sitting alone in a private booth adjoining the press box.

Competition was his passion. Lombardi was just as intense on the golf course — his one non-football diversion — as he was trying to win NFL championships.

(Top) One of Lombardi's first — and most brilliant — moves when he took over the Packers was moving former quarterback Paul Hornung (5) to halfback and using him as a run-pass threat. Here Hornung looks to throw toward Boyd Dowler as Fuzzy Thurston (63) stands guard.

No one can say Lombardi blamed others for his rare defeats. When the previously unbeaten Packers were overwhelmed by Detroit on Thanksgiving Day 1962, Lombardi said immediately that it was a coaching defeat and he was responsible.

There have been jokes about that, like Henry Jordan's oft-repeated line: "He treats us all the same — like dogs." But Lombardi truly was without prejudice, perhaps because he'd felt some anti-Italian barbs along the way.

Listen to Willie Davis, the Hall of Fame defensive end and co-captain whom Lombardi practically stole in a trade with Cleveland:

"I think we had a closer relationship than he had with some players because a lot of the things I had to live with, the desires, the things that were important, they were things he had lived with in his life.

"There were many times when I'd go in his office and he'd close the door and we'd have a really deep philosophical discussion. He'd talk about the parallels of his situation and mine.

"He felt that because he was Italian, he'd been held back for a long time and that's the way it was for Negroes now. He said, 'If you really want something' — and he felt I did — 'you can have it if you are willing to pay the price. And the price means that you have to work better and harder than the next guy.'

"He was not bitter when he talked about his past. I think he used it with me to show that he had great empathy for the problems of blacks all over."

Davis, by the way, became an extremely successful businessman after his playing career. And in 1984, at a reunion of the Super Bowl I team, he admitted to Kramer that, when something particularly good happens to him, he catches himself thinking of Lombardi and saying: "Coach would be pleased."

Despite all his accomplishments, Lombardi did make mistakes and was willing to admit them. The minor goofs — which would happen to anyone in a business with such revolving personnel — involved misjudging players.

No one is quite sure why, but Lombardi never liked athletes with long necks. Maybe he'd been a short, stocky guard too long himself. Whatever, a long neck was what kept the Packers from drafting safety Paul Krause one year — a shame, since Krause became a perennial All-Pro.

A far more serious error was Lombardi's decision to walk away from coaching after the '67 season. He was physically whipped, mentally exhausted and perhaps struck by the notion that, having won three straight championships, there were no more mountains to climb.

After turning over the job to Bengtson, his defensive coordinator, Lombardi tried to settle in as a no-meddling general manager. But he missed the action. Missed it something fierce.

Former Packer great Tony Canadeo, by then one of the club's broadcasters and a close friend, remembers the agony.

"He (Lombardi) just had to go back to coaching again," Canadeo said. "He felt lost up in that press box. He was the type of general who couldn't fight a war from his desk.

"He had to be down on the field with us, with his people, yelling, 'What the hell is going on out there?' That was it right there — 'What the hell is going on out there?' You could hear him up in the press box."

Thus Lombardi had to reverse course and leave Green Bay. He

Lombardi with his first Packers coaching staff — (from left) Norb Hecker, Bill Austin, Pat Peppler, Red Cochran, Phil Bengtson and Tom Fears.

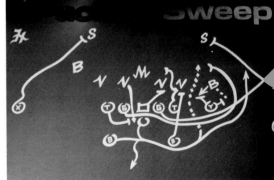

couldn't undercut Bengtson, so the only recourse was coaching somewhere else.

Before he left for Washington, Lombardi thanked the people of Green Bay for all their kindnesses and said, "I'll always be your friend."

All over football, Lombardi clearly left an indelible impression — not only on the game itself, but on an awful lot of the people who played it. And those who knew him well admired him immensely.

All of which gave Green Bay its second dynasty — there was nothing shabby about Curly Lambeau's six league titles and 29 straight winning seasons, remember — and made the Packers an international symbol of athletic excellence.

About the only question Lombardi left unanswered is how he would have worn over the long haul. As autocratic and discipline-oriented as he was, could he have survived and succeeded as football, and people, changed so dramatically around him? Some recall the Ringo incident — trading a star in a matter of minutes because he retained an agent — and propose that the world might have left Lombardi in its wake.

No one close to the Packers agrees. In fact, almost everybody who

The Packers and Vince Lombardi always will be linked — historically and emotionally. When the legendary coached died of cancer in 1970, members of his old team stood in respectful silence prior to a game in Milwaukee.

played or worked for Lombardi believes he would have been a winner in any era, in virtually any profession.

As a coach? No doubt.

"He might not have liked the way things are now quite as much," Thurston said, "but I guarantee you he was smart enough to adjust and succeed.

"And he'd probably be making about $4 million a year. Because there's nobody better."

Yet another Hall of Famer, linebacker Ray Nitschke, summed it up another way.

"I'm still amazed, when I go around the country, how people still want to talk about our teams, how they remember everything. You know what it is? It's the aura. Lombardi gave his teams an aura.

"He made us proud, and believe me, we're still proud." ❖

Chapter 3

Served with Ice

*"It was probably the most famous play in the most famous game ever played. And
only one of the 11 guys who ran it knew what was going on."*

— Ken Bowman

No matter how many years pass, conversation about the Packers' greatest glories somehow always returns to one special point in time.

When a football team has won 11 world championships and been involved in so many dramatic, historic battles, it ought to be downright difficult to single out the most memorable.

But it isn't.

Yes, the Packers have played for titles in remarkable circumstances, in various settings and with assorted results, since the 1920s. They've participated in some spectacular shootouts — remember that Monday Night Madness, 48–47 over Washington in 1983? And that same wild season, Green Bay locked up in no less than five overtime thrillers, an NFL record.

Despite all that, despite achieving triple championships twice — a feat no other franchise has accomplished even once — and despite the fact that Green Bay won the first-ever Super Bowl, the one game all Packers fans remember most is easy to pick.

Just ask anyone in Wisconsin and surrounding environs — for that matter, ask football enthusiasts from anywhere else — and the odds are pretty good they can recite chapter and verse just exactly where they were and what they were feeling on December 31, 1967.

Pack rooters who weren't even born in '67 act as though they were, because everyone knows about the Ice Bowl.

Footing was bad that day, but Bart Starr managed to get this pass away. Dallas defensive end George Andrie (66) did manage to dislodge one ball from Starr and carry the fumble in for a touchdown.

"People come up to me all the time and talk about where they were sitting, what it was like and everything," current Packers quarterback Brett Favre said. "In Green Bay, that game will always seem like it happened yesterday. I'm getting used to it. I'm one of those people who wasn't even alive then, but now I feel like I was at the Ice Bowl, too."

And so that's precisely where any recap of huge games in Packers history surely must start. Right there, a foot from the goal line, as Bart Starr stood freezing along with everyone else in 13-below weather, preparing to take a snap from center with 16 seconds to play.

It was, of course, the NFL championship game against Dallas — a showdown to determine whether or not Vince Lombardi's final Packer team would advance to Super Bowl II and keep alive its dream of winning a third straight title.

The two things almost everyone recalls so vividly about that game for the ages were the weather — so brutal that league officials consulted doctors before deciding to go ahead and so dangerous that several players suffered frostbite — and Starr's now-famous sneak for the precious few inches that provided a 21–17 victory.

"I've answered more questions about that one play than probably everything that happened in my whole career," Starr said. "Even now, people ask about that sneak in the Ice Bowl."

But in reality, there were some amazing moments which led to the final play — including a steely-eyed gamble by the normally conservative Lombardi.

The Ice Bowl was really three games in one.

The Packers coasted through the first, ignoring the temperatures, the rapidly freezing turf and all the Cowboys' fury. Starr heaved 8- and 43-yard touchdown passes to Boyd Dowler in the first half as Green Bay zoomed to a 14–0 lead while the shivering Cowboys seemed lifeless and totally out of it.

Then matters turned drastically upside-down.

Dallas defensive end George Andrie pounced on a Starr fumble and lurched 7 yards for a touchdown. The usually sure-handed Willie Wood bobbled a punt, setting up Danny Villanueva's 21-yard field goal that cut the margin to 14–10 at halftime.

The Cowboys, who lost the title game the previous year at home when Tom Brown intercepted Don Meredith's desperation, fourth-down pass to preserve Green Bay's 34–27 victory, were a proud team, as well. Now they were proving it, stuffing the Packer offense and taking a 17–14 lead on the first play of the fourth quarter when Dan Reeves pitched a halfback option pass to Lance Rentzel, a play that covered 51 yards and left the crowd of 50,861 even colder.

All of which brought the Packers face to face with destiny — on their own 32-yard line with 4:54 remaining and out of second chances.

"I know I was thinking, 'Well, maybe this is the year we don't make it, that it all ends,'" guard Jerry Kramer said. "But I know that every guy made up his mind that if we were going down, we going to go down trying."

Starr felt far more upbeat.

"That was the point that our mental conditioning took over," he said. "You have to remember that we were a supremely confident team. When we got the ball that last time, I got in the huddle and you could see the look on the face of every player. There was that gleam in their eyes.

"I didn't say one word. I didn't have to.

"In the course of a ballgame, you don't really have time to reflect on things that have happened up to that point, but I do feel we felt responsible for the tough situation we were in. My fumble gave Dallas one touchdown and Willie Wood's fumble gave them a field goal, so our defense really hadn't given up anything except that one long play. I know that definitely crossed my mind."

The last drive was textbook stuff. Even though he was having trouble gripping the ball because of the cold, Starr began throwing passes that were magnificently conceived even if not aesthetically gorgeous.

Running backs Donny Anderson and Chuck Mercein — the latter a mid-season pickup who wasn't able to stick on anybody else's roster — made brilliant decisions running routes against the Cowboys secondary and kept getting themselves open. Starr found Anderson for healthy gains when the Dallas linebackers dropped deep and then, when the

It wasn't just the fumble. Between two first quarter scoring marches and the final, famous drive, Starr was hounded by the outstanding Cowboy pass rush.

The Packer defense was contested, trying to stop a Dallas attack that included slashes — and one big pass — from Cowboys running back Dan Reeves (30).

Even the minus-13 temperature and brutal winds couldn't keep the Lambeau Field faithful from storming the field to celebrate the Packers' dramatic 21–17 victory over Dallas in the Ice Bowl — the 1967 NFL championship game.

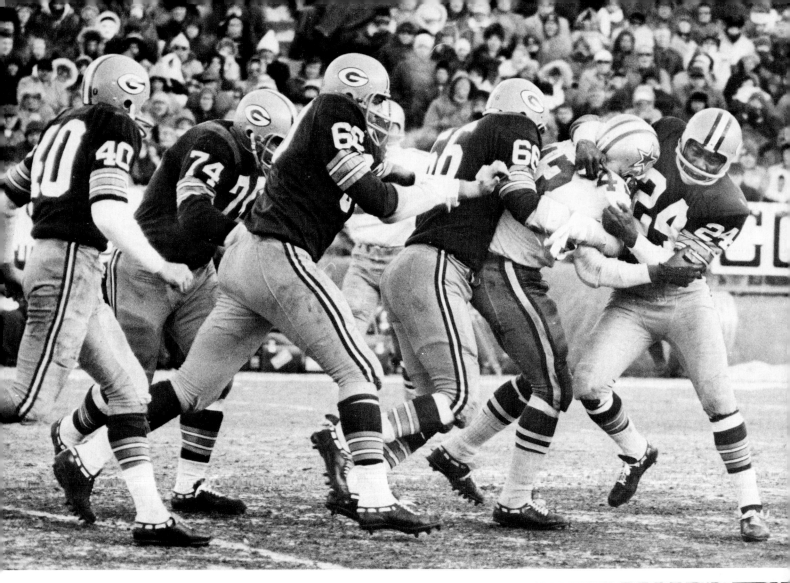

backers closed to the middle, he dumped off to a wide-open Mercein near the sideline.

"Chuck and Donny were both very intelligent, very alert players who could read what the coverage was giving us and find the open spots," Starr said. "Chuck came back to the huddle after one play and said the linebackers were ignoring him and he'd be open if we ran the same play. We did, and he was."

But the clock kept ticking.

After the two-minute warning, Starr hit Anderson for nine yards, then Mercein for 19 and a first down on the Dallas 11. The crowd was in full howl by this time, no matter the wind-chill.

"Right then, I made the best play call of my life," Starr said. "We hadn't run a 'give' play all day. We'd been saving it and this was the time."

The idea was to prey on the quickness of Dallas tackle Bob Lilly, who was relentless in his pursuit along the line of scrimmage. The play called for left guard Gale Gillingham to pull to his right — presuming that Lilly would read that key and follow him. Mercein would then hit the vacant hole, assuming the unblocked Lilly was gone and that left tackle Bob Skoronski could hold his block on right end Andrie.

"Lilly committed himself right away and chased the guard," Mercein said. "You either run right behind the guy or he gets you because nobody

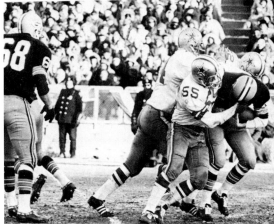

Most of the time on that frigid day, the defenses dominated. Runners fighting for traction on the frozen turf usually were buried before they could get going.

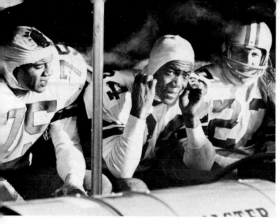

Sure, they were shivering on the outside, but Lombardi (right) and Dallas coach Tom Landry were burning with the hunger to win.

(Right) Chuck Mercein, a midseason pickup, became a big man in the Packer backfield in the Ice Bowl. This reception near the sideline put Green Bay in scoring position during its last-gasp march.

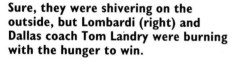

blocks him. I think if I'd had a little better footing, I might have been able to drive the last couple of yards."

As it was, Dallas' Mel Renfro dragged him down on the 3-yard line. The Packers were in range of an easy field goal to tie the game, but with 54 seconds left, they were going for the win.

Anderson scuffled forward for a couple of yards and first down on the next play, but then on two more tries, he barely got back to the line of scrimmage. On the second of those carries, Anderson slipped and nearly fumbled before being engulfed about a foot from the end zone.

So Starr called time out — the Packers' last — with 16 seconds left. Decision time.

The Packers had plenty of options, but the situation was fraught with danger. They could try the field goal, the safest course although with the footing so treacherous, Don Chandler's kick wouldn't quite be a cinch. Or they could pass, leaving them another play for the field goal if nobody was open and Starr had to unload the ball.

Or they could shoot the works. Run it again. And be out of time if they fell short.

There have been dozens of versions passed around about just what went on when Starr reached the sideline to meet with Lombardi. And what happened afterward.

The truth: Starr came off the field convinced that a wedge play would work. That blocking scheme called for Kramer and center Ken Bowman to double-team Dallas tackle Jethro Pugh, who had been a tough man to move all day. But Starr also suspected the call he liked and felt totally confident about — 31-wedge, a dive by fullback Mercein — might be trouble because of the conditions.

"The scoreboard at that end of the field casts a huge shadow," Starr

said. "If it's possible, that spot was even harder than the rest of the field. As I'm telling this story right now, I'm sitting at a granite table, and I can knock on this granite and tell you the field was every bit as hard as this table.

"I decided that we had a better chance if I kept the ball instead of giving it to Chuck. Our backs were having problems slipping around. I was right up there at the line of scrimmage, where I could kind of wiggle my feet a little for traction and just lunge forward. I asked our offensive linemen if they could get enough footing to block for the wedge play, and they said they could. That's what I told Lombardi."

And the reply?

"I remember exactly what he said," Starr recalled. "He told me: 'Then run it and let's get the hell out of here.' That was it, word for word."

Starr didn't exactly share all his information in the huddle, though. He decided not to tell anyone that he'd be keeping the ball.

"Bart called the 31-wedge and we all thought Chuck would get it," Bowman said. "Even Chuck thought so. Bart was the only one out there who knew what he was going to do."

And what he did, of course, was squeeze into the tiny crack opened by Kramer and Bowman, who managed to get Pugh standing straight up with no drive left in his legs to jam up the play.

Perhaps the biggest play of Green Bay's winning drive in the Ice Bowl was Mercein's 8-yard burst up the middle that put the ball on the Dallas 3-yard line. Starr has often said that the play call was the best of his illustrious career.

The most famous play in NFL history: Starr wedges a foot into the end zone with seconds remaining to win the Ice Bowl and send the Packers off to Super Bowl II and a chance for their third consecutive world championship.

In the victorious Packer locker room, emotions poured out after the Ice Bowl. A happy Lombardi gushed his gratitude to one and all, while Starr seemed almost dumbstruck at what his magnificent team had accomplished.

(Right) Even the Packers admitted they weren't keyed up for Super Bowl II againt Oakland — not after the emotional Ice Bowl triumph. But Green Bay survived, in part because linebacker Ray Nitschke (66) made it his business to stuff Raider runners like tough Hewritt Dixon (35).

Oh, and crazy as it sounds, at least two Packers weren't even watching this moment on the brink. Defensive tackles Henry Jordan and Ron Kostelnik had turned their backs and headed off toward a more comfortable place to wait.

"There's nothing we can do now," Jordan told Kostelnik. "Let's go get warm."

Maybe they were so used to winning that they just assumed something good would happen. If so, they were right.

"I knew it was a touchdown as soon as the ball was snapped," Starr said. "It was really easier than it looked once those guys got the block. But look at pictures of that play. You'll see Chuck Howley, Dallas' outside linebacker, on top of me just over the goal line. Do you realize how hard and how furiously he had to be closing from the outside to get all the way in there?

"That was a tribute to the Cowboys, and how they played. They were a great, great team. That's one thing that made the Ice Bowl so famous, I believe. It wasn't just the weather or us going for three straight championships or the last drive.

"It was the fact that you had two truly great teams. That brings out the best in everybody."

And the outcome brought out chaos as the fans — frozen stiff but utterly delirious — rushed the field and somehow clambered atop those stone-cold goal posts.

Once in the locker room, the Packers seemed to realize that they had pulled together one more time, one spectacular time, and produced a comeback that was the stuff of legends.

Another running back nobody else wanted, Ben Wilson (36), started and starred in Super Bowl II.

(Left) The Packers put their famous sweep to good use against Oakland, with Starr handing off to Donny Anderson as guards Gale Gillingham (68) and Jerry Kramer (64) prepared to clear a hole.

"Everybody was in tears," linebacker Ray Nitschke said. "Of all the moments I've ever seen around a football team, that was the greatest. A lot of the love that Coach Lombardi talked about was evident there. There was a great feeling of respect for each other.

"The jubilation afterwards was not a loud, boisterous thing. It was just a quiet, rewarding, satisfying feeling. You were numb because of the cold, but more numb because of what you accomplished. I'm glad I was part of that moment.

"I had frostbite in both of my feet, which I discovered the next day, but I didn't realize it, I was so numb in the joy of accomplishment."

Lombardi naturally was quizzed repeatedly about the decision to run the ball instead of taking a safer route, and at first he laughed it off with a joke.

"I didn't figure all those fans sitting up in the stands in minus-13 weather wanted to sit through sudden death (overtime)," he said. "You can't say I'm without compassion, although I've been accused of it."

More to the point, Lombardi believed all along that the Packers — *his* Packers — could gain a foot when it meant a football game, conditions be damned. Like Starr, he probably didn't even think the 31-wedge was that much of a risk.

But Lombardi let the gambler's image stand.

"And all the world loves a gambler," he said, "unless you lose."

There were a couple of postscripts to the Ice Bowl that fans tend to forget. It was Lombardi's final game on the sideline at Lambeau Field, for one thing. He'd already decided to retire from coaching, so he knew before it was even run that Starr's sneak would be the last — and perhaps signature — play of his incredible tenure with the Packers.

The other thing that gets lost in most reveries concerning the Ice Bowl is that, although it gave the Packers their third straight NFL title, everything still could have gone down the drain if they'd lost Super Bowl II to the Oakland Raiders a couple of weeks later in Miami.

Although Oakland was stubborn despite its own mistakes, the Packers finally blew the game open in the third quarter when Herb Adderley (26) raced 60 yards to score with an interception. That's Ron Kostelnik (77) out looking for someone to block.

The final ride: Two of the best linemen ever to play pro football carred Lombardi off the field at the conclusion of Super Bowl II — Forrest Gregg (left) and Jerry Kramer.

(Top) Before the Packers could qualify for the first-ever Super Bowl in 1966, they had to survive with a 34–27 victory at Dallas in the NFL title game. Tom Brown clutched an interception of Don Meredith's desperation pass with seconds remaining, snuffing out a final Cowboy drive that had reached the Green Bay 2-yard line.

(Bottom) History about to be made: The Packers were tight and tense as they were introduced prior to Super Bowl I, prepared to defend the honor of the NFL against the upstart AFL and its first representative in that game — the Kansas City Chiefs.

Recall, also, that the Packers had reached deep for a 28–7 victory over a very gifted Rams team a week before the Ice Bowl — meaning that Lombardi's beat-up warriors had to play and win two of their toughest and most meaningful games back to back.

"I've never been around a flatter football team than we were preparing for that Super Bowl," Starr said. "We'd used up so much emotion that there was hardly anything left to give, and it showed. We were awful trying to get ready for Oakland. I don't think we even started to come around until the Thursday before that game."

Even Lombardi seemed to be caught up in the lassitude, and that's saying something. Normally short-tempered, difficult or even downright irascible before big games, Lombardi acted exceedingly gracious to one and all during the stay in Miami — jocular at press conferences, relatively easy-going at practice.

Looking back, it's obvious: He'd already been to the mountaintop and seen the view.

Almost on cue, the Packers were quite a bit less than awesome for a long time in the Super Bowl. They benefited from several Oakland mistakes to inherit a 16–7 halftime lead, but they were committing gaffes of their own — the type of errors that had become almost unheard of through the Lombardi era.

It was at halftime of the Super Bowl that the subject of Lombardi's likely retirement came into focus. Everyone had heard hints or just plain guessed that the coach would be stepping aside, but with two more quarters to play against an Oakland club that possessed some scary weapons, the Packers decided it was time to dig down one last time.

Kramer said it aloud in the locker room: "Let's just play thirty more minutes for the old man."

So they did, breaking the game open on Herb Adderley's 60-yard touchdown return with an interception and cruising to a 33–14 triumph that put the words Packers, Lombardi and dynasty all in the same sentence for good.

The victory over Oakland — anticlimactic or not — also locked the Ice Bowl into a special place forever. The duel of New Year's Eve 1967 became not only one of the best and most exciting games ever played, especially considering the conditions, but because of what followed, it remains one of the most significant since it launched the Packers to their ultimate goal, the third consecutive world championship.

As heart-stopping and almost unbelievable as the Ice Bowl was — and it's hard to imagine anyone challenging those descriptions — the Packers played a game just one year earlier that someday may be viewed by football historians as even more important: Super Bowl I.

To understand what that one was all about, you have to know some history of the American Football League and what it meant to the entire sport. Conceived in 1960 as a direct competitor to the long-established NFL, the fast-growing AFL once had been considered no more than a minor annoyance.

When AFL representatives first approached NFL commissioner Pete Rozelle about staging a game between the two league champions, Rozelle was more insulted than intrigued. And he sneered: "Go get a football."

Though the first Super Bowl turned into a 35–10 Packer victory, the game was fraught was tension. One of the coolest customers on the field, veteran wide receiver Max McGee, turned into an unlikely hero with two critical touchdown catches.

But the AFL hung on and improved steadily, in part by throwing big dollars into the fray and signing away proven NFL stars — not to mention blue-chip college prospects. One scheme concocted by the upstart league was particularly effective: AFL teams decided to pool their money in an attempt to hook most or all of the NFL's big-name quarterbacks.

So finally, the NFL had no choice but to cave in, accept the inevitable and sue for peace. A merger was stuck that provided for championship games — it hadn't been named the Super Bowl just yet — after the seasons from 1966 through 1969, interleague exhibition games beginning in the summer of '67 and, ultimately, full-scale partnership in 1970.

To say that the NFL brass accepted this deal is not saying they liked it. Many old-line owners and administrators were bitter and resentful. And one of the most furious was Vincent T. Lombardi — a traditionalist if football ever knew one.

"Nobody, absolutely nobody, hated the AFL more than Vince Lombardi," longtime Packer wide receiver Max McGee said. "It was a slap at everything he stood for."

Considering the big picture, then, the eventual NFL-AFL collision in Super Bowl I became enormous when at last it appeared on the horizon. No one knew what might happen when teams from the two leagues actually stepped onto the same field — or how the game itself might be skewed when they did. So as the 1966 season wound toward its finale, media hype began revving up to a fever pitch.

The Packers discovered soon enough that the Chiefs, with savvy Len Dawson at quarterback, were better than anyone had expected.

Yes, Lombardi was worried about the Chiefs. Here he confers with defensive coordinator Phil Bengtson.

Two Hall of Famers collide: Willie Davis gets in on a tackle of Otis Taylor, the Chiefs' dangerous receiver.

If there is such a thing as a game in which one team has everything to lose and the other everything to gain, this would be it. That fact wasn't lost on NFL people, either, who first of all wanted — no, demanded — a victory in Super Bowl I and fervently wished that it might be an ungodly blowout.

That kind of pressure easily might have unraveled a normal team — even an exceptionally good normal team — but the NFL caught a huge break because, even though Lombardi's Packers perhaps weren't quite as talented and fearsome as they'd been in the early '60s, they were still outstanding. Not to mention prepared for any sort of pressure by their indomitable coach.

Lombardi wanted victory every Sunday and said as much, but there's no question he wanted it more than ever down the stretch in '66. He made it plain — and told his players — that Green Bay should be the NFL's first representative to face the new league. Deserved it, in fact.

The Packers zoomed to the Western Conference title that year with a 12–2 record, winning their last five regular-season games — although every one of them was close. Still, onetime star Paul Hornung had been almost no factor all year because of a pinched nerve in his neck, an injury that ended his career. Elijah Pitts, relatively untested except for several seasons of outstanding special teams play, had stepped in as Jimmy Taylor's running mate in the backfield.

As it turned out, offensive execution was not the problem in the NFL championship game at Dallas. The Packers, using a completely revised scheme, befuddled the Cowboys with 367 yards of total offense and raced away to leads of 14–0 and — midway through the fourth quarter — 34–20.

But defense *was* a problem.

The Cowboy offense rolled up 418 yards against a Packer unit that had yielded 23 points just once all year. When Meredith threw a 69-yard touchdown pass to Frank Clarke to make it 34–27 and Dallas promptly got the ball back, the chance for overtime looked downright ominous.

Meredith immediately ushered his Cowboys back to the Green Bay 2-yard line, but Dallas jumped offside.

"When we're leading 34–27 and Dallas has a first down on the 2, we're terrified," Packers wide receiver McGee said. "There's nothing we can do but pray.

"We haven't stopped the Cowboys all afternoon and we know they're going to score and the game is going to overtime. If that happens, we're dead. Dallas had momentum and we're emotionally exhausted.

"Then somebody in the Cowboy line jumps offside and we're saved. To me, we won that game because of Vince Lombardi. Lombardi discipline was the difference. Nobody who played for Lombardi would ever have jumped offside and cost the club a ballgame or a championship.

"He wouldn't have permitted it."

Even with the penalty, the Cowboys still might have scored, but on fourth down, Meredith was chased toward the sideline by linebacker Dave Robinson and had to throw in desperation. Brown squeezed the interception at the back of the end zone and Green Bay was headed to Super Bowl I.

Thus the stage was set for the NFL's reigning dynasty to defend the

(Above) Starr was pressured hard and often by the bigger Chiefs, especially in the first half. But the Packers later returned the favor as Willie Davis and Lee Roy Caffey (60) sacked Dawson.

(Left) When Green Bay finally did take second-half command of Super Bowl I, it was with grinding defense and the power running game keyed by Jim Taylor (31).

league's reputation against the Kansas City Chiefs — a gifted young team that had bombed Buffalo in the AFL title game. And Lombardi, naturally, took center stage.

The first Super Bowl was scheduled for January 15, 1967, at the Los Angeles Memorial Coliseum. The media hordes that descended on southern California in a pregame feeding frenzy, however, found that Lombardi had sequestered his Packers 90 miles north in Santa Barbara — where he was flogging them with almost maniacal fervor.

"We didn't know a thing in the world about Kansas City," Hall of Fame offensive tackle Forrest Gregg said. "We had never seen them play except on TV. And Vince came out and talked to us. Our first meeting. And he left no question in our minds that they had a great football team.

"He said, 'You look at the size of the people they have and you look at the reputation they had before they got into pro football and then you watch them on film and you are going to be convinced that you are going to be playing a good football team.'

"He scared us to death. He really did."

For Lombardi, though he realized his Packers should actually dominate the game, truly was scared himself. The prospect of being upset by an AFL team unnerved him.

CBS broadcaster Frank Gifford recalled doing a live pregame interview with Lombardi at the Coliseum and that the Packer coach was shaking so badly, he had to grip Gifford's arm.

"It was the only time I ever saw Lombardi that tense and up tight," Nitschke said. "He was so tense and nervous about everything, he made us tense and it carried over into the game — which is something he *never* did.

"I really believe Lombardi's mentality before that Super Bowl affected us so much that we played poorly in the first half. But it was more than that. We were nervous and the Chiefs were good. They were even better than we'd thought they'd be. Heck, look at the players they had — Lenny Dawson at quarterback, Bobby Bell and some others. And three years later, they won the Super Bowl, so they were definitely tough and very well coached by Hank Stram."

The old reliable sweep wore down
Kansas City's defense. This time it was
Elijah Pitts (22) lugging the ball.

Packers defenders, meanwhile, snuffed out all of Kansas City's upset hopes by shutting out the Chiefs in the second half.

A touch of irony from Super Bowl I: Chiefs defensive back Fred (The Hammer) Williamson had vowed to knock out several Packers with his vicious forearm slash, but instead he wound up belted woozy himself after catching a knee to the head from runner Donny Anderson.

The first half of that historic clash must have been a nightmare for the NFL's old guard. The Chiefs outgained the Packers 181 yards to 164 and trailed just 14–10. Worse yet, their huge defensive line — led by another future Hall of Famer, Buck Buchanan, had hounded and pounded Starr.

"They were as big and tough as we feared," Starr said, "and they gave me some lumps. But they did have some weaknesses in their pass defense, and we knew if we could just settle down and play, we could exploit them."

McGee was the game's unlikely hero, and the Packers might have been in deeper trouble at halftime without him. McGee, who hadn't played much all year, found himself in the game almost immediately when Boyd Dowler went down with an injury.

And McGee opened the scoring with one of the most unbelievable touchdown catches in Super Bowl history, a 37-yarder from Starr that Max admitted later he was simply trying to knock down because Starr had been nailed as he released the ball and it was frighteningly off course — at least two feet behind McGee.

"Let's face it, it was a rotten pass," McGee said later, laughing at the memory. "You pay a guy a hundred thousand dollars to throw to a 25-thousand dollar end, you expect him to throw better than that. I wasn't going to go back and get killed by some linebacker. I thought sure somebody was going to intercept the ball, so I reached back to knock it down, to break up the interception — and when I did, the ball stuck in my hand. Just like that. Stuck right in my hand."

McGee caught the ball on the 19-yard line and then, when cornerback Willie Mitchell fell down lunging for him, lugged the thing for the first-ever Super Bowl touchdown.

"It was an accident," he said.

The Packers, though, could not count on accidents all day — and in the second half, they didn't. Instead, they got back to Lombardi football, dominating the line of scrimmage, forcing mistakes and capitalizing on them.

The game turned on the first series of the third quarter when, with the Chiefs still fired up and driving, Dawson was rushed into a quick throw that was intercepted by Wood, who scooted 50 yards to the Kansas City five-yard line.

Pitts scored from there on the next play to make it 21–10 and order had been restored.

"Willie Wood probably would have made it to the Hall of Fame anyway," Dawson said years later, "but I probably helped put him in by throwing that pass. I've seen it on so many replays and it still looks just as bad."

Green Bay overwhelmed the Chiefs for a 35–10 victory after that pivotal turnaround, getting another short TD dash from Pitts and McGee's second remarkable scoring catch — a 13-yarder that he juggled as he was hit and once more hauled in one-handed.

"I've had better days," McGee said, "but I never timed one better."

There was an unusual windup to all the tumult in Los Angeles. Delighted as he was to have defended the prestige of the Packers — and the entire NFL — Lombardi did something which made him very unhappy with himself.

Besieged by reporters to compare Kansas City with the Cowboys and other NFL clubs, Lombardi had tried to duck the question, but finally he said: "The Chiefs are a good team but they don't compare with the top teams in the NFL. Dallas is a better team. That's what you wanted me to say, isn't it? Now I've said it."

But Lombardi, always the professional and a man who insisted on giving respect as well as demanding it, felt terrible about caving in on the comparisons.

"I came off as an ungracious winner and it was lousy," he said.

Better, however, than as a loser — especially in a game that meant so much.

The two Super Bowl triumphs, with those back-to-back battles with Dallas thrown in for sheer drama, probably constitute the Packers' best-remembered stretch of games. They occurred during the time TV first was beginning to swamp America's living rooms with pro football, for one thing, and they put a powerful exclamation point on the Lombardi era.

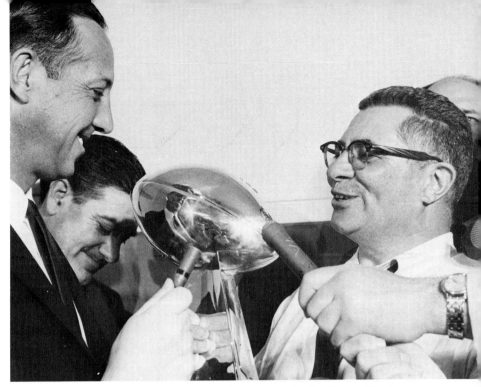

Lombardi accepts the Super Bowl trophy — which now bears his name — from NFL commissioner Pete Rozelle.

But the Green Bay franchise has been involved in so many, many more epic games that — standing by themselves — easily could be crated and shipped to Canton.

They go way back, to the Packers' first championship season in 1929. There was no divisional play then, just one league and one winner, but there *was* a title game. The Packers, who finished 12–0–1, had to beat the mighty New York Giants (13–1–1) at the Polo Grounds with four weeks left in the regular season.

And they did it, 20–6, as Bo Molenda threw for one touchdown, ran for another and Johnny "Blood" McNally sewed up the win with a final TD.

That victory proved that the onetime town team from rural Wisconsin could prevail against the big boys — even on the road — and when Curly Lambeau's Packers returned to Green Bay, cheering crowds nearly overran the train station with a resounding welcome home.

Consider another moment of pure theater, on a day that previewed one of the greatest careers the NFL has ever seen.

In the second game of 1935, Arnie Herber threw an 83-yard touchdown pass to beat the Chicago Bears 7–0. The recipient was Don Hutson, a rookie from Alabama who went on to record the league's first 100-yard receiving day later in the season and caught six touchdown passes that year. Hutson ultimately hauled in 99 TD throws, a record which stood for 44 years.

There were certainly plenty of other monumental games in the Lombardi era, too, including a 37–0 thrashing of the Giants in the 1961 championship. It was Lombardi's first title and also the first that the Packers ever won in Green Bay instead of Milwaukee, where most of their showdowns had been scheduled in previous years.

Tight end Ron Kramer drags a pair of Giants toward the goal line.

(Right) Running back Tom Moore cuts toward daylight as the Packers play one of their best games ever in swamping the Giants for that '61 title.

The scoreboard told the story as the Packers swamped the Gaints for the 1961 championship — the first time they'd ever won one at home in Green Bay.

Who can forget that Western Division playoff heart-stopper with Baltimore in 1965, the game that saw the Colts open with halfback Tom Matte forced into the quarterback spot because of injuries to Johnny Unitas and backup Gary Cuozzo — and finished in overtime after perhaps the most hotly debated field goal the NFL has ever seen?

The Packers were big favorites for one play, or until Starr threw an interception for a touchdown on the first play from scrimmage. Starr hurt himself trying to tackle thundering linebacker Don Shinnick, so Green Bay's No. 2 quarterback, old reliable Zeke Bratkowski, became the man of the hour.

The Colts easily could have won the game 10–7 on the strength of their bruising defense, but Bratkowski led the Pack into field goal range late in the game and Don Chandler kicked a 22-yarder with 1:58 remaining.

The 1965 Western Division playoff with Baltimore got off to an ominous start when Starr (at top) injured his ribs on the first play from scrimmage.

Starr's absence made a hero of backup quarterback Zeke Bratskowski (12), who saved the Packers on several occasions and did it again this time in crucial circumstances.

Baltimore had its own quarterback problems in this famous overtime duel. With Johnny Unitas and backup Gary Cuozzo hurt, running back Tom Matte stepped in under center with the plays written on a wristband. Here Matte confers with coach Don Shula.

Or did he?

To this day, nobody is quite sure whether or not Chandler's kick — which sailed high above the upright — snuck just inside the post or was wide to the left. Don Shula, who has won hundreds of games since but was coaching the Colts that day, still bristles at the mention of Chandler's boot.

Good or not, the field goal counted and Green Bay won 13–10 in overtime on Chandler's down-the-middle shot from 25 yards — but only after Baltimore's Lou Michaels missed a 47-yarder that almost sucked the air right out of Lambeau Field.

The veteran Chandler conceded afterward that the whole turn of events was almost too much for him. "I was shaking like a leaf," he said.

For utter bravery in a pit of violence, some Packer partisans might remember 1962 and the 16–7 league championship victory over the

(Top) Colts kicker Lou Michaels could have won the game in overtime, but his field goal attempt slid wide.

(Bottom) The kick that won it: Don Chandler boots one straight through the uprights, handing Green Bay a 13–10 triumph and a date with Cleveland in the 1965 NFL championship game.

The 1962 showdown was a war fought in cold, windy conditions and decided by a brutal battle in the trenches. Fullback Jim Taylor was pounded again and again by the Giants, but he toughed it out to lead the Packers' running game.

Giants in New York — on a bitterly cold day that reduced both teams to brutal trench warfare.

Green Bay's winning margin came from three field goals by Kramer, who was recruited for kicking chores because Hornung — the league's leading scorer from 1959–61 — had been injured early in the year.

The relentless Jim Taylor, hammered so hard by Giants linebacker Sam Huff early in the game that he swallowed blood the rest of the afternoon, somehow ground out 85 yards and cemented his reputation as one of the toughest hombres ever to lug a football.

Guard Jerry Kramer was an unlikely scoring hero as the Packers defeated the Giants 16–7 in New York for the 1962 title. With regular kicker Paul Hornung out with an injury, Kramer connected on three field goals — the exact margin of victory.

"You look back and you know that you had nothing left — nothing — and yet you still continued to play," Taylor said. "No one knows until they are faced just how much pain they can endure, how much suffering, how much effort they have left. The coach stepped in and pushed a player beyond that point. That's the way it was that day."

Huff was stunned by his foe's ability to keep going.

"Jimmy Taylor can't be human," he said.

Does it seem like the Packers were always running into those fearsome Giants in high-stakes games? Back in 1944, Lambeau won the

The Packers always seemed to be playing for championships under adverse conditions. Lambeau Field was a muddy quagmire as they whipped Cleveland 23–12 to win their first title in three years in 1965. Boyd Dowler (86) ignored the slop and slippery football to make a big catch.

The Packers' biggest games were played in all sorts of weather extremes. If it wasn't flirting with frostbite, it might have been a matter of dealing with blazing sunshine. Ray Nitschke (right), who was frozen numb a year later in the Ice Bowl, actually had to take some oxygen during steamy Super Bowl I in Los Angeles. But that was the Green Bay code: Ignore the weather and win anyway.

last of six titles when the Packers survived a 14–7 test of wills in New York as Ted Fritsch scored two first-half TDs and the Green Bay defense made it stand up with two late interceptions — against former Packer Herber, of all people.

That was the game that prompted Hutson to say: "If I ever play another game in New York, I'll jump off the Empire State Building."

The latter-day Packers have played some biggies, as well, even if thereweren't championships at stake.

A nation of TV viewers may *still* be spellbound by the Monday Night marathon of 1983. There's really never been anything else quite like it in prime time.

It was that season Lynn Dickey threw for a club-record 4,458 yards — not to mention 32 touchdowns — and the Packers scored 429 points while leaking an equally stunning 439. Even by the up-and-down, score-and-score-again standards of '83, though, the 48–47 victory over the Redskins for a Monday Night Football audience was something to behold.

The offensive orgy that evening including 11 TDs, 11 conversions and six field goals. Jan Stenerud's 20-yarder with 54 seconds remaining won it, but just for added drama, Washington's Mark Moseley missed from 39 yards on the final play.

"I wish I'd been in the stands or watching on TV," Dickey said. "It's the wildest game I've ever been in."

Try this: Starr, who was coaching the Packers for his ninth and final season, seemed awed by the entire affair. "I've never been involved in a more exciting game," he said.

Forgive Bart if the Ice Bowl slipped his mind for second.

The Packers have played so many memorable games, even a Hall of Famer's thrills can start to run together. ❖

Chapter 4

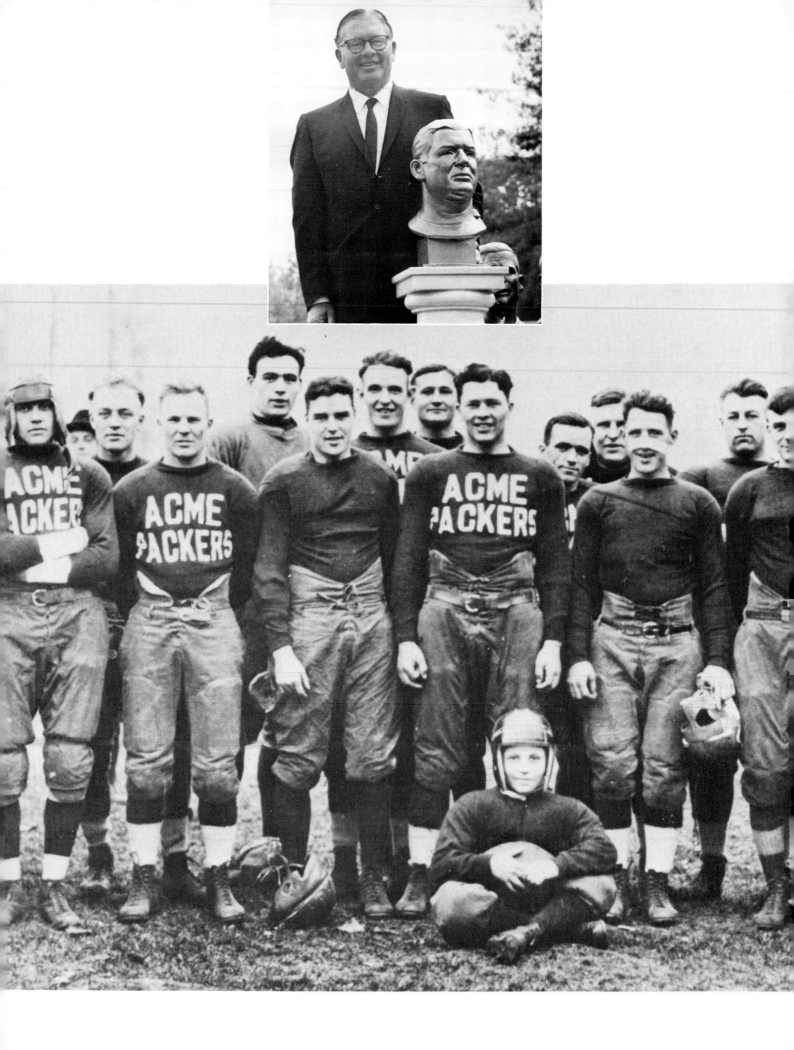

Curly and Cal Meet for a Beer

"Why not get up a team in Green Bay?"

— George W. Calhoun

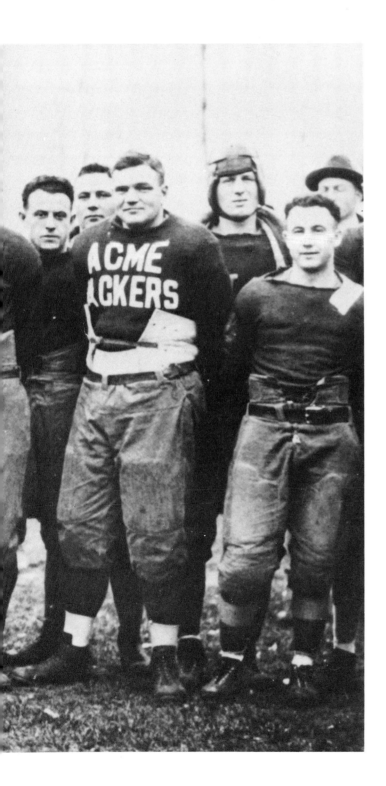

Fans of the TV age perhaps think that the Packers sprung suddenly to life under Vince Lombardi, that nobody in Wisconsin had ever seen a first down until the 1960s.

Not quite.

To say that such latecomers are missing a remarkable, glorious era in Green Bay football history would be a spectacular understatement. In fact, as awesome as Lombardi's decade of dominance might have been, it certainly can't compare to the longevity of Curly Lambeau's reign as Mr. Packer.

Nor even come close.

No disrespect to the revered Lombardi, who won five championships and never had a losing season with the Pack, but Lambeau first scraped this franchise together with nickels and dimes in 1919, then roared through a stretch of 29 years with just one losing record and six world titles of his own — not to mention revolutionizing the young NFL with the forward pass and instituting the game's first-ever daily practice sessions.

Lambeau also played halfback during the first decade of his tenure, proved a positive genius as general manager by continually upgrading his team's personnel and stepped forward repeatedly as the front man battling tough odds to keep the financially strapped organization solvent.

Fitting, then, that Curly was one of the inaugural inductees into the Pro Football Hall of Fame when it

(Top) The Packers were a "town team" before they became true professionals. This is the first team, Curly Lambeau's 1919 outfit.

Huge lineman Cub Buck was one of Green Bay's early stars — later, he became a Hall of Famer.

opened in 1963. He went 212–106–21 as head coach, one of only five men in league history to win 200 games or more.

John B. Torinus, longtime member of the Packer executive board and author of a club history that was published in 1982, offered a succinct and telling description of Lambeau: "He was a man among men."

And, yes, Lambeau had a lot in common with the gentleman who resurrected his dynasty, Vince Lombardi.

"They were both so dedicated and they were both disciplinarians," said Tony Canadeo, who became a Hall of Fame running back for Lambeau in the 1940s and later — as a fixture in the Packer family — a very close friend of Lombardi's. "These were two men who demanded that things had to go their way, period.

"Lambeau ruled the roost just the way Lombardi did later on, and Curly did it for a long time. He could put fear in people, believe me. Both Lambeau and Lombardi were exactly the right men for their eras — just the way I think Mike Holmgren is just the right coach for the Packers in this time.

"But don't think Lambeau or Lombardi would have been left behind at any time in the development of football. People like that could have adjusted and fit in any era."

Lambeau and Lombardi had something else in common, too, which was perfect for the heroic roles they were asked to play. Both had egos just slightly smaller than Lake Michigan and reputations that were larger than life.

There is plenty of evidence that Lombardi, who outshone everyone in pro football during his run, felt just a little uncomfortable knowing that he had a predecessor right there in Green Bay whose accomplishments were every bit as legendary.

Lombardi fretted and fussed over having his picture taken with Lambeau in 1961 — when the Packers were busy regaining the NFL's highest throne. Then in '65, when Lambeau died, Lombardi fumed

outright that the same picture appeared on that season's cover of the Packer yearbook. Lambeau might have cast the only shadow in sports under which Lombardi felt any noticeable shade.

As for Lambeau, he was a peacock — a snappy dresser, ladies' man and high-stepper of the first rank. Curly enjoyed the limelight and felt at ease with the media. The more, the merrier. He relished those early, history-making trips to New York City and likely would have been a television dandy if he'd come along later in the evolution of the game.

But just in case anyone is still clinging to the notion that the Packers only reached the big time with the arrival of Lombardi, club public relations director Lee Remmel — who saw both men in their heydays — offered a reminder.

"There couldn't have been a Lombardi if there hadn't been a Lambeau, at least not in Green Bay," Remmel said.

Actually, there probably wouldn't be any Packers in Green Bay, either, since Lambeau not only created the team out of his own iron will, he kept it going when small-town teams all over the map were succumbing to fiscal woes — either folding outright or moving to bigger cities.

Oh, and another, truly local twist: There probably wouldn't have been the Lambeau Packers or anybody else's Packers if there hadn't been a George Whitney Calhoun.

Too bad there isn't a place in the Hall of Fame for characters like Calhoun, who really shared in the fathering of professional football in Green Bay. And that's a heck of a story in itself.

Of course, so was Calhoun.

Cal was the sports editor of the *Green Bay Press-Gazette* back in '19 — a cigar-chewing curmudgeon with an ill temper and very little patience toward foot-draggers or anyone else he felt was interfering with his goals of the moment.

Beer drinker extraordinaire, hard-driving newspaperman, late-night companion for a lot of truly interesting souls and a tireless champion of local teams and athletes, Calhoun was famous for perching his pooch — Patsy Toosie Tiger — on the next bar stool and holding court until all the world was right as he saw it.

But Cal was more than just another crusty old hack from the pages of

(Top) Spectators came all decked out for Packer games at Hagemeister Park in 1919.

Was this tailgating before its time? Fans jammed cars around Hagemeister Park every Sunday.

(Left) The start of a rivalry: The Packers and Chicago Bears going at it in 1923.

(Above) Center Jug Earpe, another Packer hero, was related to legendary lawman Wyatt Earp.

(Right) The best quarterback in the Packers' first decade, Red Dunn, looked for yardage in a 1928 game. Note backfield mate Eddie Kotal, playing without a helmet.

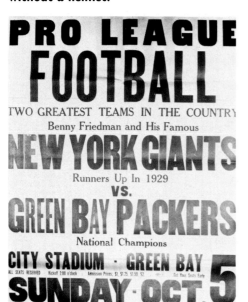

a Damon Runyon novel. He worked himself numb creating the Packers out of the city's needs and energies — as he saw them — and almost literally beat the drums until the Packers were known nationwide.

Before any of that could occur, though, the community had to have a team in the first place. Lambeau and Calhoun, who later would use very different methods and skills but who were both hungry for the same result, cooked up the franchise over a stein of beer.

Which really shouldn't have been a surprise at all.

The whole wild tale began when Lambeau, who had been an all-sports star at East High in Green Bay, came home after one semester at Notre Dame. He'd already made the varsity for immortal coach Knute Rockne, but Curly suffered a serious bout of tonsillitis. He probably intended to return to South Bend — and what almost certainly would have been sure stardom — but doctors back in Green Bay told him they couldn't operate until he'd shaken the infection which made him so sick.

So after Christmas 1918, Lambeau was still back home. And he never left.

By late summer that year, Curly was already missing football, and one night when he and Calhoun were out throwing down a few cold brews, Lambeau admitted the passion continued unchecked. And that's when Calhoun suggested the novel idea of building a team right there in Green Bay.

Cal promised powerhouse help from his newspaper, and he made good. And then some.

Here's what Calhoun wrote after the first meeting of prospective players, a gathering at which Lambeau — naturally — was chosen as captain:

"Curly Lambeau, former East High and Notre Dame football star, was elected captain of the Indian Packing Corporation's team at the meeting last night of city footballers at the *Press-Gazette*. G.W. Calhoun will again manage the eleven this season.

"Close to 25 pigskin chasers attended the conference last evening and there was a good deal of enthusiasm displayed among the candidates. It was the unanimous opinion that, if Green Bay doesn't get away with state honors this year, she never will.

Johnny (Blood) McNally was not only a triple-threat player who helped the Packers win championships from 1929–31, he was one of football's most colorful characters on and off the field.

(Left) A tradition that still holds: The first Packer band poses in 1927.

"Practice will start September 3, the Wednesday following Labor Day, and from then on it will be held three times weekly — Mondays, Wednesdays and Fridays."

That might have brought forth Calhoun's first official word on the Packers, but it was far from his last. Later on, when history came calling, Cal and his trusty typewriter were ready for full-time duty.

Since money was never in suitable supply in the early days — or for decades to come, matter of fact — it was a fortunate turn of events that Lambeau had a first-year sponsor right on his doorstep. When he chose not to return to Notre Dame, Curly went to work at Indian Packing for $250 a month, a sizeable amount at the time and enough to keep him from caring much about a college education.

Lambeau cadged jerseys from his boss, Frank Peck, and even a practice field next to the plant. So even though the Indian Packing Corporation was absorbed soon after by another company and Calhoun's first team nickname — the Indians — never quite stuck, football was off and running in Green Bay.

Technically, the Packers weren't exactly professionals their first two seasons. Players split all profits, which came to the princely sum of $16 per man in 1919. They didn't join the fledging American Professional Football Association — soon to become the NFL — until 1921, but it was fun right from the beginning.

For one thing, at a time when teams simply knocked heads and ran the football in what was little more than brutal trench warfare, Lambeau already was in love with the passing game. That didn't exactly endear him to some opponents, who thought throwing the ball was a cowardly approach to a man's sport.

In one game against a rugged club from Stambaugh, Lambeau watched three of his players suffer fractures on consecutive running plays and decided enough was enough. So much for bravado.

"I never called another running play," he said, "but after every pass I had to run for my life. Those (Stambaugh) miners were tough."

Perhaps gearing up his prose for later glories — including three straight world championships from 1929–31 — Calhoun hit stride as quickly as the fledgling team.

Very few fans could make it to road games, so they gathered around the "Playograph" in Legion Park. Scores and updates were relayed from other sites before the advent of radio.

A pre-Lombardi Packer sweep: Bobby Monnett turns the corner.

The Packers were the first pro team to make extensive use of film study in preparing for games. Coach Curly Lambeau (rear left) presided over the projector in 1948 along with assistant coaches (front, from left) Tom Stidham, Bob Snyder and Charley Brock. That's Hall of Fame receiver Don Hutson, by that time a member of Lambeau's staff, at the coach's side.

The Packers won their first 10 games in 1919, outscoring the opposition 565–6, but then they were upset in the season finale, 6–0 by the oddly named Beloit Fairies. The game was in Beloit and the result was exceptionally suspect, since the hometown referee disallowed Packer touchdowns on three consecutive plays late in the game to preserve the victory.

Calhoun was outraged and wrote with a vengeance:

BELOIT, Wis., Nov. 24 — *The Green Bay Packers met defeat at the hands of the Beloit Professionals at Morse Park on Sunday by the score of 6 to 0 before a good-sized crowd of spectators.*

Capt. Lambeau's team was robbed of victory by referee Zabel of Beloit. This official penalized Green Bay three times after touchdowns, refusing to allow the scores. The Packers were twice on the verge of leaving the field but decided to play it out.

Every time the Packers had the ball, the crowd would sweep out on the playing field, leaving practically no room for the forward pass offensive and, of course, in this way, putting a big check on the Packers' ground gaining machine.

Just before the close of the game, McLean got away for a long run, headed goalward, close to the sidelines, when a Beloit spectator gave him a foot and the Green Bay quarterback fell to the ground.

And so on.

Things became a little less chaotic once the Packers joined the soon-to-be NFL in 1921, but even then, there were moments of high anxiety or delicious irony.

For instance, after Green Bay went 7–2–2 in '21 and opened the game's longest-running rivalry with a 20–0 loss to the Chicago Staleys — they became the Bears a year later — the league decided to revoke the Packer franchise because Lambeau had used some college players in violation of previously unenforced by-laws.

By then, the Packers had become the property of the Acme Packing Company. So Don Murphy, one of Lambeau's pals whose brother was

an Acme investor, accompanied Curly to the 1922 league meeting. The idea was to offer an apology and try to get Green Bay reinstated.

The league accepted the apology, sure enough, but also asked for $250, which was the cost of renewing a franchise. The two men didn't have that much in their pockets, so Murphy sold his car on the spot to provide the up-front money. And so the Packers actually belonged to Lambeau himself until 1923, when the team first became a corporation and stock was sold to the public.

Murphy became a footnote on the playing field, as well. As payback for unloading his vehicle, Murphy got Lambeau to promise that he could play in the 1922 season opener.

And he did, lining up with the kickoff team against the Duluth Eskimos. But Murphy was no fool. He quickly headed to the sideline before encountering any contact, preserving his good health while landing himself in the books as having played in an NFL regular-season game.

The Packer franchise itself nearly had just as brief a stay.

The club scuffled financially in 1922, and may only have survived because of a rainstorm. Actually, there were two famous rainy days that year — the first costing the club a lot of money because the amount of rainfall was one-hundredth of an inch shy of what was necessary for a payout by the Packers' insurance company.

Then another squall, before a game the Packers were scheduled to

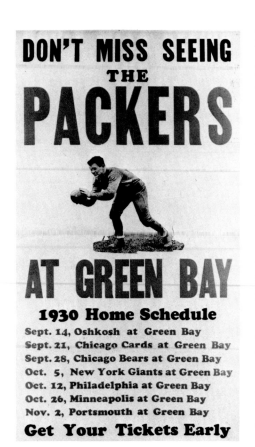

DON'T MISS SEEING THE PACKERS

AT GREEN BAY

1930 Home Schedule

Sept. 14, Oshkosh at Green Bay
Sept. 21, Chicago Cards at Green Bay
Sept. 28, Chicago Bears at Green Bay
Oct. 5, New York Giants at Green Bay
Oct. 12, Philadelphia at Green Bay
Oct. 26, Minneapolis at Green Bay
Nov. 2, Portsmouth at Green Bay

Get Your Tickets Early

play against Duluth at home, probably saved the team from going out of business. Lambeau and Calhoun were at the *Press-Gazette* office that Sunday. If they went ahead with almost no paying spectators, they would be stuck for the guarantees they owed the Eskimos.

Andrew B. Turnbull, then the newspaper's business manager, came to the rescue. He first told Curly and Cal that, if they ever hoped to make Green Bay a true professional franchise, they had to play. But Turnbull also promised to advance the guarantee money himself and round up investors for a stock sale the following off season.

Lambeau, Turnbull and three other local businessmen — Lee Joannes, Dr. Webber Kelly and Gerald Clifford — became known around town as the "Hungry Five" for their efforts finding investors to keep the Packers afloat prior to the 1923 season. That stock sale, however, became the cornerstone of the Packers — and the basic structure of the corporation remains intact today.

Fiscal problems aside, the Packers were a good football team right from the beginning. Lambeau had also been a solid player but he was even better at finding talent and acquiring it.

Starting with giant tackle Cub Buck, who came on board in 1921, and all-purpose back Verne Lewellen from the University of Nebraska (1924), Lambeau kept adding star-quality athletes who could not only keep Green Bay competitive in the NFL, but eventually put the Packers atop it.

The huge leap finally came in 1929, which might have been a rough year for the stock but was strictly a blue-chip season for Packer football. Lambeau added two future Hall of Famers — tackle Cal Hubbard and guard Mike Michalske — to the roster that year and landed another star who was possibly the most colorful player of the NFL's early days, halfback Johnny "Blood" McNally.

In his college days, the gifted McNally and some of his chums often picked up walking-around money by playing for a pro team on Sunday. Since that practice had been formally outlawed by the NFL, many players simply used assumed names.

McNally and a friend were walking past a theater one day and noticed on the marquee that the feature was *Blood and Sand,* a movie starring lady-killer Rudolph Valentino. "That's it," McNally told his pal. "You be Sand, and I'll be Blood."

So it was Johnny Blood who appeared on the Packers roster through some of the team's most successful years.

In addition to drinking and chasing women, at which he was definitely an All-Pro, McNally could run, kick and pass — but he was also an outstanding receiver coming out of the backfield, something of a rarity at that time.

It's awfully difficult to compare players from totally different eras, but the similarities between McNally and future Packer Hall of Famer Paul Hornung seem inescapable. Both were multi-talented guys, toughest in big games and championship settings — and both spent a lot of time out in the middle of the night.

Also like Hornung decades later, McNally was surrounded by emerging talent in 1929 and for awhile afterwards. Along with the 250-pound

Greeting champions has become a Green Bay habit. Fans swarmed to the Washington Street train depot to welcome home their heroes after a victory in the 1944 title game.

Hubbard and rock-steady Michalske, all-purpose back Bo Molenda joined Green Bay in '29 when the New York Yankees franchise folded. That trio filled out a cast that Lambeau already had made exceptionally strong.

Curly previously had added center Jug Earp, end Lavvie Dilweg, quarterback Red Dunn, end Tom Nash, guard Whitey Woodin and back Carl Lidberg to the roster, so the only surprise about the 1929 season was that the Packers not only won their first world championship, but that they went undefeated (12–0–1) while doing it.

And while titles have always been welcome in Green Bay, the '29 team provided something almost more delicious when they shut out the Bears — it was already a blood-boiling rivalry — three times. The last of those three victories came in Chicago, and when the Packers headed home, cheering fans lined the railroad tracks for five solid miles between De Pere and downtown Green Bay.

Lambeau had the nucleus of a great team, and proved it with three straight championships — a feat accomplished only once more in NFL history, by Lombardi's teams from 1965–67.

In fact, with the addition of new heroes like quarterback Arnie Herber, end Milt Gantenbein and bruising fullback Clarke Hinkle, the Packers almost made it four in a row in 1932. They were 11–1–1 at the end of November — ties didn't count in the standings — but lost twice after that, to Portsmouth and then 9–0 to the Bears in a vintage Chicago blizzard.

Lambeau, meanwhile, had retired as a player right in the middle of the triple titles. He stepped off the field following the '29 season, having thrown 24 touchdown passes in nine years — no small feat at a time when the forward pass was still finding its way into pro football.

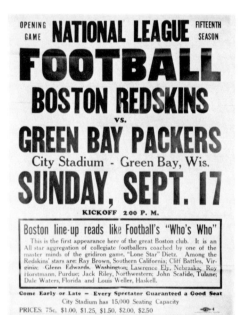

George Whitney Calhoun, sports editor for the *Green Bay Press-Gazette*, early team manager and force behind the Packers.

The Packers and the entire NFL veered onto a new course after the near-miss of '32. The league went to a two-division format in 1933, the same season that the Pack broke tradition and began playing some home games down the road in Milwaukee.

Lambeau was nothing if not adaptable, however. He changed personnel relentlessly, even after great seasons, always attempting to upgrade the team and replace aging stars. As the key players from the triple championship era departed, new talent arrived — in particular Don Hutson, who hit the league like a ton of bricks in 1935 and soon was setting records that stood for half a century.

So the Packers kept winning. They endured their only losing season in Lambeau's first 29 years at the helm in 1933, then promptly regrouped to win another title in '36 as Herber threw touchdown passes to Hutson and Gantenbein in a 21–6 victory over the Boston Redskins. That one was particularly sweet since the Packers had been bombed 30–3 by the Bears at home on the second Sunday of the season — while Blood was holding out for more money — then rebounded to win 21–10 at Chicago late in the year.

The Packers suffered their first of only two championship-game losses in 10 tries in 1938 when they lost 23–17 to the Giants in New York, but again they bounced back to win it all in 1939 by hammering New York 27–0 at Milwaukee — starting another tradition of surviving in bad weather when they were forced to ignore 35-mile per hour winds at State Fair Park.

Lambeau's final championship came along in 1944, with an entirely different cast that included running back Ted Fritsch, who scored twice in a 14–7 title-game showdown at New York.

Curly Lambeau's long tenure was remarkable, indeed, but it had its unpleasant times, too.

For instance, after Lambeau had become famous around the country, he apparently decided he no longer needed the services of his old crony, George Calhoun. The way he did it was even colder: Calhoun was reading the Associated Press teletype machine one morning in 1945 and found a dispatch announcing that Lambeau had hired Chicago sportswriter George Strickler as the Packers' new publicity director. Furthermore, it said, Calhoun was retiring.

Sadly, Calhoun became Lambeau's foe rather than friend after that episode. And Cal wasn't alone, either, as several members of the original "Hungry Five" discovered along the way that Curly had become too much of a one-man band for their liking.

All that business came to a head in the late 1940s, when disappointments began cropping up at an alarming rate. The Packers at last were losing games, for one thing. They were 3–9 in 1948 and 2–10 in '49.

And they were losing money, in part because Lambeau — now having gone completely Hollywood in the locals' minds — purchased the infamous and expensive Rockwood Lodge as club headquarters and brought in his new wife from California to decorate their own personal cottage with costs of no concern.

The clash of Lambeau's ego and the franchise's long-term health at last came to a head following the disastrous 1949 season. The executive

Coach Curly Lambeau (center) — a man among men.

committee ordered Curly to cut some players and renegotiate the salaries of others, dismissed Strickler the PR man and ordered that Rockwood Lodge be put up for sale.

Ultimately, the lodge went up in flames before it could be sold — a financial godsend — but the fire might as well have been licking at Lambeau's future in Green Bay, as well.

Remember that 1949 was also the year that fiscal problems forced a Thanksgiving Day exhibition game that hopefully could keep the team afloat, and after the season, the committee decided that another stock sale was an utter necessity.

Lambeau responded by telling the committee that he knew four investors who would be willing to put up $50,000 apiece — on the condition that the Packers be restructured as a for-profit enterprise. In fact, Curly was trying to buy the team as a business venture, but he was rebuffed when the committee stuck to its guns and refused to alter the team's non-profit status.

All Lambeau gained from those tumultuous gatherings was a grudging two-year extension of his contract as coach and general manager, but apparently he never had any intention of fulfilling those duties. Soon after the attempted power play to gain control of the

Old City Stadium, adjacent to East High, was expanded several times until the capacity reached 25,000. Eventually even that wasn't enough seats and the new City Stadium — now Lambeau Field — was built in time for the 1957 season.

franchise, Lambeau resigned to become vice president and head coach of the Chicago Cardinals.

In almost any other setting, you'd think that would have been the last the Packers would have heard from Curly Lambeau. But this was a determined man with long connections to a very special football team, and Lambeau actually sought out the general manager's position a decade later. He was rebuffed again then, too, when the executive committee handed over both the coach and GM's jobs to a man with no previous head coaching experience in pro football — Vince Lombardi.

For all the untidiness at the end, Lambeau's place in Packers history cannot be shaken. He helped bring the team to life, he kept it breathing when days were darkest and he was a winner in the grandest style — only the Bears' George Halas matched Lambeau's six NFL championships.

It is entirely fitting that now, in an era of unprecedented popularity and huge profits in the NFL, that the hugely successful and always unique Green Bay Packers play in a stadium that bears his name — Lambeau Field.

Curly Lambeau remains a man among men. ❖

Chapter 5

Battling Papa's Bears

"I'm from Chicago and I always dreamed of playing in Wrigley Field. Then when I finally did, people screamed things and threw garbage at me. But there's nothing else like the Packers against the Bears."

— Ray Nitschke

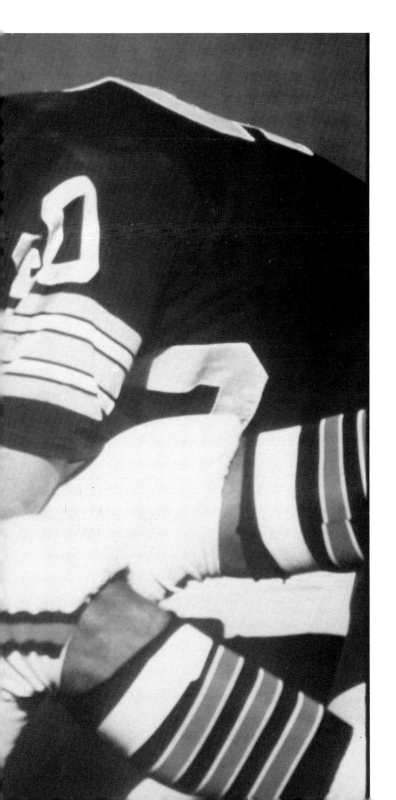

They've run and passed, hit and grabbed, clawed and scratched, bit and kicked for seven decades and change in the NFL's oldest and longest-running rivalry.

They've even prayed.

Consider one of the more recent brawls between the Packers and the Chicago Bears, that infamous "instant replay" game of November 5, 1989.

For the longest time, this particular dance was just like so many more of the 145 meetings between old, proud, fierce franchises which also happen to be neighbors with a common state border. In other words, it was brutal.

The Bears blitzed Green Bay's young quarterback, Don Majkowski, unmercifully. Middle linebacker Mike Singletary shot through the line of scrimmage on the first play of the game and the assault never let up. Majkowski was sacked five times and knocked down at least a dozen more.

"It was ugly," Green Bay offensive tackle Ron Hallstrom admitted. "Scary sometimes. At times I felt like everyone was coming up the field."

But the Packers dealt out some punishment, too. Rugged safety Chuck Cecil, who was returning to the lineup after missing eight weeks with a hamstring injury, roared up to rock Bears running back Neal Anderson so hard near the line of scrimmage that Lambeau Field actually fell silent.

Cecil took advantage of the momentary quiet to

Quarterback Don Majkowski (right) and receiver Sterling Sharpe hooked up on one of the most famous plays in the Packers' long rivalry with Chicago — the "instant replay" game of 1989.

Fans of these two franchises never miss a chance to make fun of each other.

(Right) Two of the game's immortals, Vince Lombardi and George Halas, meet at midfield before the Packer-Bear game.

perform a shimmying, quaking celebration dance as Anderson came groggily to his senses.

This sort of thing was just business as usual for the Packers and Bears, who over the years have hit each other with everything short of ball bats and tire irons. Remember, this is the rivalry that got off to a flying start in 1921 when Bears lineman Jim "Tarzan" Taylor sucker-punched Green Bay's Cub Buck and broke his nose.

So the rock 'em, sock 'em stuff was nothing new. But sometimes a Packers-Bears matchup provides added drama, and this was destined to be one of those times.

Chicago was defending a 13–7 fourth-quarter lead when the Packers mounted a last, desperate drive that featured all sorts of craziness. On first down from the Bears' 7-yard line with under a minute remaining, Majkowski was clobbered by linebacker John Roper and fumbled. Packers center Blair Bush fell on the ball back at the 14.

Two incompletions later, Majkowski was looking at fourth and the ballgame. Again he was pursued and again he fled for the sidelines, searching frantically for a green jersey anywhere near the goal line.

Suddenly, wide receiver Sterling Sharpe broke clear, slashing across the middle of the end zone. "I was waving my arms and I was hoping that Don saw me," he said. "I was just praying that no one was behind me. Don saw me at the last minute and threw a strike. Touchdown."

Or maybe not.

Before the Packers could even start a celebration, they saw the penalty flag that line judge Jim Quirk had thrown to signify that Majkowski was beyond the line of scrimmage when he released the pass. That's a five-yard infraction, but it carries loss of down — which would have handed the game to the Bears.

Ah, but at that point, the ghosts of this incredible rivalry must have stepped in. Upstairs in the replay booth, official Bill Parkinson buzzed Quirk to say he wanted to review the play.

"This was a very important play," Parkinson said later. "The ballgame hinges on this play. We took our time."

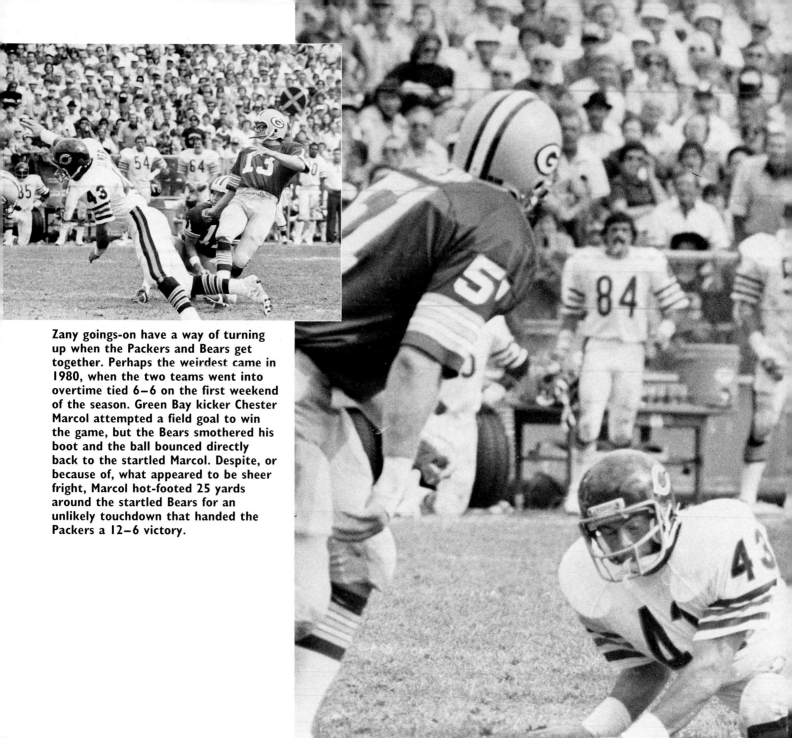

Zany goings-on have a way of turning up when the Packers and Bears get together. Perhaps the weirdest came in 1980, when the two teams went into overtime tied 6–6 on the first weekend of the season. Green Bay kicker Chester Marcol attempted a field goal to win the game, but the Bears smothered his boot and the ball bounced directly back to the startled Marcol. Despite, or because of, what appeared to be sheer fright, Marcol hot-footed 25 yards around the startled Bears for an unlikely touchdown that handed the Packers a 12–6 victory.

No kidding.

Parkinson and his assistants looked and looked, while the Lambeau Field crowd, both teams and coaching staffs went through agony. Five minutes might not seem like much in the grand scheme of life, but when you're waiting for a decision on the outcome of a Packers-Bears game, well, it's an eternity.

And time for more prayer.

"All you can really do when it goes up to the booth — because you don't know what goes on up there — is cross your fingers and say a prayer, hope everything works out right," said Green Bay offensive tackle Ken Ruettgers.

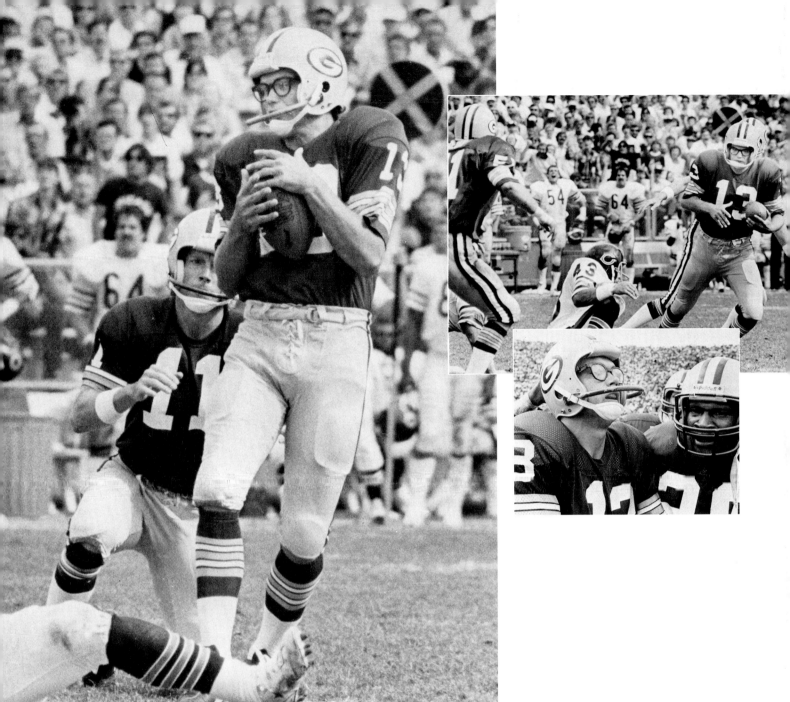

Even Bears coach Mike Ditka admitted to seeking help from an authority higher than the replay booth. "Prayer is a wonderful thing," Ditka said. "Sometimes it works and sometimes it doesn't."

This time it didn't, at least not for Iron Mike.

Referee Tom Dooley finally stepped to the center of the field, snapped on the microphone that connected him to the public address system and made the announcement: "After further review, we have a reversal . . ."

The rest was drowned out in a thunderous roar, as the touchdown was restored, Chris Jacke kicked the extra point to give the Packers a 14–13 victory and unadulterated joy swept Wisconsin.

Ditka, meanwhile, had gone from spiritual to profane. He performed

A hometown boy who returned to torment the Bears: Packer running back Tony Canadeo (3) hailed from Chicago, but he took great delight in breaking loose to make his boyhood heroes look bad.

an angry war dance on the sideline and refused to mellow afterwards — insisting that the Bears' media guide in following seasons carry an asterisk next to the result of that game. And so, right on through the 1992 season, Bears press books have denoted the 14–13 loss with the infamous asterisk and an explanation: "Instant Replay Game."

Actually, it was probably fitting that the replay cameras — now banished from the NFL after a lengthy and stormy trial period — should decide a Bears-Packers collision. Why not? Almost everything has happened to these two teams.

For utterly furious competition, these franchises had it all going from the beginning. They were close geographically, they were both immensely successful and they were run by give-no-quarter coaches who were giants of the game.

Between them, the Packers and Bears have won no less than 20 world championships — 11 and 9, respectively. There have been enough heroes in these uniforms to fill up an entire wing at the Hall of Fame — as it is, 48 players who at one point in their careers represented Green Bay or Chicago are enshrined already.

Some perhaps ought to be honored together, just for the earth-shattering wars they fought face to face — like the Packers' rugged Clarke Hinkle and Chicago bruiser Bronko Nagurski.

On the one side of this relentless regional struggle, you had George S. Halas — Papa Bear — who founded the Chicago franchise as the Decatur Staleys back in 1920. Halas was present at that historic meeting in

Canton when the NFL was formed. And he was around a long time afterwards — 63 years as a player, coach and owner.

Halas, who stepped away from coaching by his own volition four times, nonetheless was on the sidelines for six championships — a record he shares with Packers founder Curly Lambeau. Next on that list, by the way, is Green Bay's Vince Lombardi, with five titles.

So in addition to being just a few hours apart, the two clubs often were fighting for league-wide supremacy. And they've always sneered at each other while achieving it. After the Bears hammered the Pack 33–14 in a 1941 Western Division playoff game, Chicago fullback Bill Osmanski said: "Green Bay is a one-man team. You always know that if you stop Don Hutson, you should win the game."

Of course, Chicago couldn't always do that. Hutson's first of 99 pass-receiving touchdowns was an 83-yarder that beat the Bears 7–0 in 1935.

Despite the Bears' 80–59–6 overall advantage in the series, both teams have recorded huge victories that offered plenty of opportunity for gloating. And they go way, way back — Green Bay's first world title in 1929 turned mostly on the Packers' three shutout wins over the Bears.

And needless to say, things have always been rough.

"People from other parts of the country just don't realize what this game means in Wisconsin and Illinois," said Ray Nitschke, Green Bay's Hall of Fame linebacker who grew up in Chicago and attended the University of Illinois. "The Bears and Packers, that's football at its best, the way it should be.

The Bears got the best of most matchups with Green Bay in the early days — much to the delight of Packer-baiting fans at Wrigley Field in Chicago.

Papa Bear himself — Geroge Halas. The man who helped found the NFL was both friend and foe to the Packers for 63 years.

It was only fitting that Vince Lombardi's first game — and first victory — as Packer coach was a 9–6 thriller over the Bears in 1959. After that win, fans at Lambeau Field stormed from their seats to shower Lombardi with congratulations.

"The teams don't like each other at all. The cities don't, the fans don't — it's pretty intense. If the Packers have a bad game against the Bears, the whole season feels like it's lost.

"You could feel an entirely different attitude around town before we played the Bears. It was 'Bear Week.' You'd go to the grocery store and the barber shop, and everybody would be saying, 'Are you ready to go? It's the Bears.'

"As though we had any trouble being ready for the Bears. If you can't get up for that game, you shouldn't be playing. The intensity, even in the crowd, is just unbelievable."

Longtime Bears tackle Jimbo Covert agreed.

"You can be up for some games, but you'd better be ready when you play the Packers," he said. "You're playing guys in your own backyard. When you get all done playing, these are the games you'll remember most."

For all sorts of reasons.

Pro wrestling legend Dick "The Bruiser" Afflis played four seasons as

Gang tackling is always a good idea, but in a Packer-Bear game, it's a must. Chicago running back Ronnie Bull is about to be crunched by Dave Robinson (89), Lee Roy Caffey (60) and Willie Wood (24). Then Bull gets more of the same (right) from Willie Davis (87) and his friends.

a lineman for Green Bay, but his most memorable day against the Bears came after he'd left the field to make his fortune in the ring. It seems Afflis had recently married a young lady from Boston and he brought her to a Bears-Packers tiff at Wrigley Field.

The way Afflis recalls it, Green Bay was trying to rally when one of the Packers broke a long kickoff return down the sideline — past the bench where Afflis and his bride were sitting alongside the Packer players. Mrs. Afflis got so excited, she jumped up and followed the ballcarrier all the way to the end zone — naturally creating quite a commotion.

"The Andy Frain ushers who work at Wrigley Field came around and there was a big fight," Afflis said. "They threw me and my wife both out onto the street."

The six-decade relationship between Halas and his rivals to the north, meanwhile, was something to behold. It always seemed to be a love-hate thing. Halas clearly admired the Green Bay franchise from its earliest days and fought to kept the Packers in the NFL when finances were bleak. He enjoyed the company of men like Lambeau and Lombardi, but lived to pound 'em on the football field.

There's little doubt: The Packers of today probably wouldn't even exist without Halas.

Lambeau got in trouble with the league right off the bat in 1921, using collegiate players illegally. So Curly had to approach NFL owners with

The Packers and Bears have more players in the Pro Football Hall of Fame than any other teams, so there have been some classic matchups. That's Dick Butkus (51) engulfing Green Bay quarterback Bart Starr.

hat in hand prior to the 1922 season, hoping to get his disbanded franchise reinstated.

"From the very first, the league had declared its opposition to using collegians," Halas wrote in his autobiography, "but we did not enforce the rule."

So the Packers were going to be made an example.

"We revoked the Green Bay franchise," Halas said, "and demanded an apology from Curly. Fortunately, Curly found another sponsor and with cash raised by a friend who sold his car, applied for a new franchise. We supplied it."

Business between Halas and the Packers cut both ways.

In that same '22 season — after speaking up to see that Green Bay got back its team — Papa Bear refused to bring his club north because the Packers wouldn't guarantee him enough money. That was the only year until the NFL's 1982 player strike that the Bears-Packers series was interrupted. But Halas also was on the other end, once getting caught short of cash when a game in Chicago was played in a snowstorm. Gate receipts produced only $1,000 of the Packers' $2,500 guarantee, so Halas wrote out a personal note for the remaining $1,500.

Halas wasn't done helping the Packers, either. Not by any means.

In 1956, when Green Bay desperately needed a new stadium to compete in a league that was growing with the TV age, Halas came to town as a lobbyist during a huge rally for support of a city referendum.

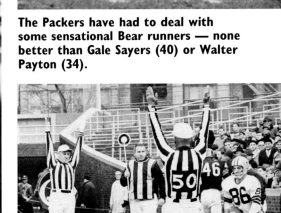

The Packers have had to deal with some sensational Bear runners — none better than Gale Sayers (40) or Walter Payton (34).

Always a pretty sight: The officials signal touchdown as Packers receiver Boyd Dowler comes up with a tumbling catch against the Bears in 1967.

Head to head: Bears runner Brian Piccolo and Packers linebacker Lee Roy Caffey brace for a jarring collision at the line of scrimmage.

So naturally, after the bond issue passed and the new stadium was built, the Packers said thanks by beating the Bears 21–17 in the inaugural game.

Halas' intervention was far more specific in 1959, when the Packers reached one of the lowest ebbs in franchise history — at least on the field. They hadn't had a winning season since 1947, and in '58, with popular but beleaguered Ray "Scooter" McLean suffering through his single year as head coach, Green Bay turned in a disastrous 1–10–1 record that sent the club's executive committee searching for somebody to turn things around.

People don't remember much of this anymore, but Vince Lombardi wasn't the only coaching candidate the Packer brass considered for 1959. In fact, he might not have been the first choice — Iowa's Forrest Evashevski was considered the frontrunner while the committee was hashing over its options.

Eventually, though, the men in charge kept coming back to Lombardi, who was an assistant coach with the New York Giants and exceptionally well regarded throughout the NFL. The only hitch was that Lombardi had no head coaching experience at any level above high school, so Packers president Dominic Olejniczak sought out Halas.

"I shouldn't tell you this, Ole," Halas said, "but he's a good one. I shouldn't tell you this because you're liable to kick the crap out of us."

Halas was a prophet, because Lombardi — more often than not — did give the Bears some serious lumps. And they weren't long in coming.

Where are you heading for dinner? Anyone with the ball is going to draw company quickly in this rivalry. Just ask Packers John Brockington (42) or James Lofton (80).

One of the most dramatic victories in Packer history came in Lombardi's first game — a 9–6 thriller over the Bears to open the 1959 season. That was the day thousands raced down from the stands in Green Bay, hoping just to touch Vince Lombardi.

There was irony aplenty that afternoon. Lombardi had insisted on a five-year contract because he claimed Packer fortunes couldn't be turned around overnight, and even after, the new coach said, "I'm no miracle-worker."

But by beating the Bears, and doing it with a fourth-quarter rally the way they did, Lombardi's Packers sent out a loud message to the football world in general: Another dynasty was brewing in Green Bay.

Talk about omens: The Packers won it with a late drive culminating in a touchdown run by Jimmy Taylor and an extra point from Hornung. It was a peek into the future.

Linebacker Bill Forester said: "He (Lombardi) ended the speech before the game by yelling, 'Now go through that door and bring back a victory!' I jumped up and hit my arm on my locker. It was the worst injury I had all year."

Listen to Hall of Fame defensive back Emlen Tunnell, whom Lombardi had brought along from the Giants to wind up his magnificent career: "I knew right away in that first game that we were going to be

Tough as a player, tough as a coach. Chicago's Mike Ditka (89), here pursued by Hank Gremminger (46) and Dave Robinson (89), was a rugged tight end who ran over tacklers instead of around them.

good. Not great, maybe, but good. We played tough and Green Bay teams had never played tough. They gave up. This team didn't give up.

"We won it in the fourth quarter and afterward we gave him a little victory ride. In the locker room, he was proud — oh, was he. He said, 'Well, we're on our way now.'"

It was true, obviously, but the most telling thing of all was that this milepost triumph, this victory to send the Packers on to greater glories, had been achieved against a team that proved its own toughness for more than a half-century.

The Bears.

It wouldn't have been the same against anyone else.

Lombardi and Halas developed a powerful personal respect for one another, but on the field, they became mortal enemies. And to the delight of football's true believers everywhere, they commanded outstanding teams going head to head with championships at stake for most of a full decade.

No rivalry could get much better than that.

"He (Halas) was a great friend, but he wanted to beat us more than anybody else in the league," Packers Hall of Fame runner Tony Canadeo said. "It was always rough. All the years I've been with the Packers —

Just when the Packers breathed easier at the departure of Butkus, along came Mike Singletary (50) to create more havoc for the Bears at middle linebacker. He's after Eddie Lee Ivory (40)

(Right) Packer linebackers haven't exactly been sissies, even compared to their Bears counterparts. Jim Carter (50) seems to be enjoying giving the business to Chicago's Alvin Harper.

with Lambeau, Lombardi and other coaches — I can't remember that we ever played a bad Bear team.

"Halas always had them ready to face the Packers. And on our end, why, I remember that if Lambeau caught you even smiling during 'Bear Week,' you were in trouble."

Packers star Paul Hornung told one remarkable story about the Halas-Lombardi wars.

"Here comes a knock on the door in the trainer's room, and it's Papa Bear," Hornung said. "The equipment man answers the door and he says, 'Yes, Coach, can I help you?' And he says, 'Yes, I'd like to speak to Coach Lombardi and it's very urgent.'

"This is five minutes before the game, and he walks in, and here are the two coaches by themselves. He says, 'Yes, Coach, can I help you?'

"And Halas says, 'Yeah. Vince, I just want you to know that you'd better have your team ready because we're going to kick your ass.'"

Changing of the guard: Packers new coach Mike Holmgren (left) visits with Bears boss Mike Ditka prior to the teams' annual brawl in 1992. But things turned upside down for long-dominant Bears — Holmgren was named NFL coach of the year when his young team went 9–7, while Ditka was fired after the season.

The Bears delivered a mighty insult in 1985 when they let hulking defensive tackle William (Refrigerator) Perry crash over for a 1-yard touchdown against the Packers — at Lambeau Field, no less.

Not for the faint of heart: Any loose ball draws a hostile crowd when the Packers and Bears get together.

(Right) Good weather rarely visits a Bear-Packer game. John Brockington is trying to make some yardage in the slop while being mugged by Chicago linebacker Doug Buffone (55).

Hornung figures in some other memories, as well.

The Packers won NFL titles in 1961 and '62, then surrendered the league championship to the Bears in 1963 — the year Hornung was suspended by NFL commissioner Pete Rozelle for betting on college games. Hornung had led the league in scoring three straight years and he was a critical part of the Green Bay offense.

As it turned out, the Bears went 11–1–2 in 1963 to the Packers' 11–2–1. The difference was Chicago's two victories over the Pack, so if Green Bay had won either game, Lombardi probably would have had his third consecutive title — and six in seven years instead of just five. Since one of those games was a 10–3 Bears triumph at Green Bay, Lombardi and others in the Packer family always believed that if Hornung had been available, things would have been reversed.

That issue can be debated.

There is no question about another sub-plot to the Bears-Packers squabbles, however. Starting with Bear lineman Tarzan Taylor's sucker-punch swipe at Packer Cub Buck's nose in 1921, they've treated each other with no courtesy whatsoever.

Once the Bears finally regained some dominance in the 1980s — while the Packers had hit a down cycle — Chicago coach Mike Ditka saved the ultimate insult for Green Bay.

In '85, as the Bears were on their way to a magnificent season that wound up with a victory in Super Bowl XX, Ditka let elephantine defensive tackle William "Refrigerator" Perry lug the ball one yard for a touchdown — at Lambeau Field. Perry had lined up in the backfield before, but only as a blocker.

Ditka, a career Bear if you ever saw one, just couldn't resist dealing the Packers a little extra humiliation. On the tape of the Bears' radio broadcast of that game, you can hear the announcers laughing out loud as Perry was running over Packer linebacker George Cumby.

That hurt.

And so, just a year later — with the Bears still lording it over Green Bay and the rest of the NFC Central — Packers defensive end Charles Martin took it upon himself to repay the favor. Martin wore a towel in his belt with the numbers of five Bears he hoped to disable.

He got at one of them, quarterback Jim McMahon. Martin loomed over the controversial Jimmy Mac — he was either outspoken or obnoxious, depending upon your loyalties — and body-slammed him to the rock-hard turf long after a pass had been released.

Martin's cheap shot, while perhaps not exactly considered a mortal sin around Green Bay, nevertheless was pretty far outside the rules — even for the Packers and Bears. He was fined and suspended by the league.

But violence had been traded back and forth by these unfriendly neighbors long before anyone had even heard of Charles Martin. Or even Jim McMahon.

"It was such a hatred kind of deal," former Packers end Gary Knafelc said of his experience with the Bears in the late 1950s and early '60s. "We looked forward to it all year long. It was a clipping, biting, scratching type of contest."

Nitschke believes all the back-alley stuff was inevitable.

Sometimes a sign speaks for itself. This one probably contained some meaningful message, but the condition of the banner said volumes.

"You have to remember what the teams mean to the two towns, and how the cities look at each other," he said. "They were two proud franchises, two great teams with long traditions, and the wars went way back.

"So when they got together, you had to expect that with emotions so high, everybody would be taking it out on each other. It was the spirit of what football was all about, but sure, we'd all probably get carried away in Bear-Packer games."

For all the down-and-dirty antics, though, this rivalry always has come loaded down with mutual respect. The teams beat on each other the way two brothers might scrap on their back porch.

In 1962, after the Packers buried a beat-up, undermanned Bear club 49–0, Lombardi confessed that he was haunted by pain he'd caused a great man like Halas.

In his book, *Run to Daylight*, Lombardi opened the narrative — it was a week-long diary — with this entry, dated at 3:15 a.m. Monday morning:

"I have been asleep for three hours and, suddenly, I am awake. I am wide awake, and that's the trouble with this game. Just 12 hours ago I walked off that field, and we had beaten the Bears 49–0. Now I should be sleeping the satisfied sleep of the contented but I am lying here awake, wide awake, seeing myself walking across that field, seeing myself searching in the crowd for George Halas but really hoping that I would not find him.

"All week long, there builds up inside of you a competitive animosity toward that other man, that counterpart across the field. All week long, he is the symbol, the epitome, of what you must defeat and then, when it is over, when you have looked up to that man for as long as I have looked up to George Halas, you cannot help but be disturbed by a score like this.

"You know he brought a team in here hurt by key injuries and that this was just one of those days, but you can't apologize. You can't apologize for the score. It is up there on that board and nothing can change it now.

"I can just hope, lying here awake in the middle of the night, that after all those years he has had in this league — and he has had 42 of them — these things no longer affect him as they still affect me."

Give Lombardi credit for his sensitivity. But don't think for a minute that Green Bay's raucous fans were staying up late wondering about an apology to the Bears.

Nor would they be getting one if the score had come up the other way around.

The rivalry is now 74 years old and just as white-hot and laden with grudges as ever. There's bound to be more biting, kicking and scratching right around the corner. Also championships and heartbreak.

That's just life with the Packers and Bears. ❖

(Right) The next generation of Bears and Packers will certainly carry on a long, grudge-holding tradition. Green Bay's young linebacking sensation, Tony Bennett, prepares to level Neal Anderson.

Chapter 6

Four and More

"The Packers have had so many great players that they've had to stop retiring numbers. We wouldn't have uniform numbers left."

— Equipment manager Bob Noel

The oddest thing about the long, storied history of the Green Bay Packers well might be that — three-quarters of a century and 11 world championships later only four players have had their uniform numbers officially retired.

But it's true: So many stars have performed their magic in Green Bay, including 18 in the Pro Football Hall of Fame who spent most of their careers with the Pack, that the franchise would be running out of numerals if it kept holding ceremonies and taking shirts out of circulation.

Most teams can only dream of facing such a puzzle.

You know you're part of serious tradition when simply earning election to the Hall of Fame won't keep your number off a rookie at mini-camp. Yet only Tony Canadeo (3), Don Hutson (14), Bart Starr (15) and Ray Nitschke (66) have achieved the ultimate accolade of seeing their numbers retired.

Consider that Curly Lambeau, who founded the team, played superbly for nine years and coached for 31 seasons overall, has his name on the Packers' home stadium but his uniform No. 20 is still being issued.

Household names, Hall of Famers like Willie Davis, Forrest Gregg, Jim Ringo, Jimmy Taylor, Paul Hornung, Willie Wood and Herb Adderley fall into the same category — along with early heroes like Johnny (Blood) McNally, Arnie Herber, Cal Hubbard, Clarke Hinkle and Mike Michalske.

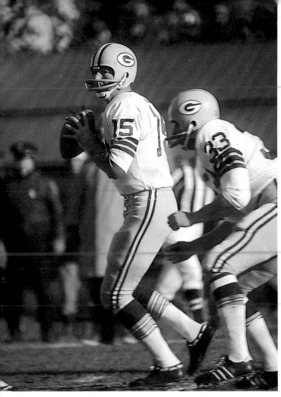

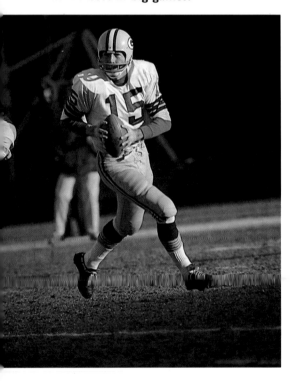

Starr often was underrated as a passer — because the Packers had such an efficient running game — but he was a deadly accurate thrower who was at his best in big games.

The Packers' overwhelming success through the years might best be demonstrated by the accomplishments of those players whose numbers *haven't* been retired. The list reads like a Who's Who in the NFL.

So perhaps it's unfair to suggest that there's such a thing as the most famous Packer of them all, but the roll call of distinction has to start somewhere — and therefore it begins with the man who overcame staggering obstacles to become one of the greatest quarterbacks the game has ever known.

Bryan Bartlett Starr.

Casual fans might reflect on Starr's remarkable career —- 24,718 yards passing with a 57 percent completion percentage, plus leadership of five championship teams from 1956–71 — and jump to the conclusion that this man was destined for greatness from the day he signed a professional contract.

Not exactly.

When Vince Lombardi took over the Packers prior to the 1959 season, Starr had already toiled through three uneventful, losing years without knocking anyone's eyes out. He'd been a 17th-round draft choice out of Alabama — a guy who hardly played as a college senior when a new coach went entirely with newcomers — and he'd spent most of his early professional days on the bench.

Later, Lombardi would get credit for seeing something special in this 6-foot-1,200-pounder. But at the beginning, Lombardi checked out Starr's skills and was as skeptical as his coaching predecessors.

In fact, Lombardi identified quarterback as one of the Packers' glaring weaknesses and so, even after Starr had led Green Bay to the 1960 title game, the coach was intensely interested in trading for Dallas' Don Meredith.

Starr had missed a wide-open receiver in the 17–13, championship-game loss to Philadelphia and afterward, Lombardi remarked: "Yeah, some guys see them and some don't. I'd like to get that guy Meredith."

No offense to Dandy Don, who was a pretty fair quarterback himself, but maybe the best thing that ever happened to the Packers during the Lombardi era was that the Cowboys turned down an offer of any two players on the Green Bay roster for Meredith.

Soon enough, Starr began to spot receivers everywhere and, under Lombardi's tutelage, he came to grasp the entire concept of offensive football — to the point where Starr now is considered one of the best field generals in football history. His poise, steadiness under fire, recognition of defenses and ability to rise up at moments of crisis carried the Packers to dynasty status.

"It's not true that I was lacking confidence when I got into pro football," Starr said. "I really did believe in myself and honestly believed that I'd make the Packers as a rookie, even being drafted in the 17th round.

"The next couple of years, sitting on the sidelines while the team was losing, definitely dampened things a bit. But I never doubted that I had the ability if I got a chance to play and learn — and to improve in all aspects of it."

Even under Lombardi, Starr had to watch as Lamar McHan

quarterbacked the team through most of the 1959 season. But Bart seized the starting job by the time the Packers got rolling toward their first division title under Lombardi in '60.

Then Starr — often playing hurt, yet always playing under control — proceeded to start a dizzying run toward the Hall of Fame, making Lombardi look even more like a genius in the process.

In some ways, though, Starr never got quite as much credit as he deserved. Cynical football people claimed he was a robot, merely executing an offense already primed to succeed — a product of Lombardi's system more than a talented quarterback who learned to read the coach's mind and then use his own gifts to produce points, victories and championships.

Once the Packers had stormed from behind to win the Ice Bowl in 1967 and set up a fifth title in seven seasons, however, Starr felt ready to step up and put the record straight.

In his autobiography, Starr said: "Earlier in my career, many fans misinterpreted my calm demeanor for lack of imagination. They believed that Lombardi programmed me to follow his orders and not worry about originality. But by the time we executed our winning championship drive (in the Ice Bowl), I had become a creative and confident leader who could stand beside, not behind, our admired coach."

That's a fair judgment. You don't make as many outstanding decisions and razor-sharp throws over such a long stretch without the touch of greatness.

"Every time Bart stepped into the huddle, we all just assumed that something good was going to happen," guard Fuzzy Thurston said. "That's just the way he was, the feeling he inspired in everybody."

There was an unfortunate side to such expectations. Everyone in Green Bay watched Starr knock down obstacles so often that he seemed to be invulnerable, impossible to defeat. That sort of reasoning led to the public clamor that pushed Starr into the Packers' coaching job in 1975.

Pride was becoming a memory. The Pack had scraped up just one division title since Lombardi's final season in '67, and the perception in Wisconsin was that only the great Bart Starr could restore his team to glory.

"I wasn't ready to be a coach," Starr conceded long afterwards. "I didn't have the experience and we didn't have the kind of solid, veteran team where you could win and learn as you went. It was difficult."

And then some.

Starr lasted nine years in the job, fighting to rebuild the Packers, and felt he'd become a pretty decent coach by the time he was dismissed following the 1983 season. So the whole situation became very unpleasant — fans at last grumbling about their once-untouchable icon and the club's executive committee feeling pressured to move in another direction.

"It wasn't the happiest time," Starr said, "but nothing can change my feelings or my loyalty to the Packers. I'll always be Green Bay's biggest fan. I'll be excited all over again when the Packers get back to the Super Bowl."

Whatever dent the coaching letdown might have put in Starr's almost

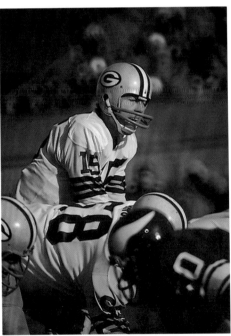

After his first few years in the NFL, no one ever questioned Starr's leadership or play-calling. He was a master running the Packer attack — whether finding the right spot for a give to Paul Hornung (5) or surveying the defense to exploit a weak spot.

(Above) The sight of Nitschke struck terror into the hearts of ballcarriers, and he wanted it that way. Nitschke often said he wanted offensive backs to have dreams about him — not necessarily pleasant ones, either.

(Right) The Big Three: Linebackers Dave Robinson (left), Nitschke and Lee Roy Caffey discuss things on the sideline.

Intense, relentless, angry in pursuit and always ready to hit: Ray Nitscke was rightfully voted the best middle linebacker in the NFL's first 50 years.

man to stop him? You're big enough and strong enough, but can you do it?"

He did it.

Brown was held to 50 yards on 12 carries — and dropped an apparent touchdown pass — as the Packers won 23–12 to reclaim the league title after a two-year drought.

"You know that pass Brown dropped in the end zone?" offensive tackle Bob Skoronski said. "He had it in his hands but Nitschke was all over him, just hustling and hollering and screaming at him."

Even Brown grudgingly paid his respects.

"I noticed that Ray Nitschke was keying on me," Brown said. "He's as tough as anybody is."

What a perfect way to sum up Nitschke's career: He was as tough as anybody.

The other two Packers whose numbers have been retired pre-dated the Lombardi era: Don Hutson and Tony Canadeo. But that pair did have something in common with the big-name stars of the 1960s: Both played on teams that won NFL championships — Hutson in 1936 and '39, Canadeo in 1944.

Hutson was almost a revolutionary in the sense that he turned pass-receiving into an art form — not to mention a frightening offensive weapon — at a time when most pro teams still believed you could only win championships by running the football.

The numbers are staggering for any age, but considering that Hutson arrived in the NFL in 1935 when passing games were still terribly unsophisticated, some of his records boggle the mind.

How about 99 touchdown catches in 11 seasons? By current standards, that seems more like 200. Those 99 scoring receptions weren't matched for nearly a half-century.

Hutson caught 488 throws for 7,991 yards in his career, despite being covered by everyone except the other team's water boy. And remember, those were the days of drastically shorter schedules.

You can make the case that no one player ever dominated pro football for a decade the way Hutson did from 1935–45, which is saying quarterbacked the team through most of the 1959 season. But Bart seized the starting job by the time the Packers got rolling toward their first division title under Lombardi in '60.

Then Starr — often playing hurt, yet always playing under control — proceeded to start a dizzying run toward the Hall of Fame, making Lombardi look even more like a genius in the process.

In some ways, though, Starr never got quite as much credit as he deserved. Cynical football people claimed he was a robot, merely executing an offense already primed to succeed — a product of Lombardi's system more than a talented quarterback who learned to read the coach's mind and then use his own gifts to produce points, victories and championships.

Once the Packers had stormed from behind to win the Ice Bowl in 1967 and set up a fifth title in seven seasons, however, Starr felt ready to step up and put the record straight.

In his autobiography, Starr said: "Earlier in my career, many fans misinterpreted my calm demeanor for lack of imagination. They believed that Lombardi programmed me to follow his orders and not worry about originality. But by the time we executed our winning championship drive (in the Ice Bowl), I had become a creative and confident leader who could stand beside, not behind, our admired coach."

That's a fair judgment. You don't make as many outstanding decisions and razor-sharp throws over such a long stretch without the touch of greatness.

"Every time Bart stepped into the huddle, we all just assumed that something good was going to happen," guard Fuzzy Thurston said. "That's just the way he was, the feeling he inspired in everybody."

There was an unfortunate side to such expectations. Everyone in Green Bay watched Starr knock down obstacles so often that he seemed to be invulnerable, impossible to defeat. That sort of reasoning led to the public clamor that pushed Starr into the Packers' coaching job in 1975.

Pride was becoming a memory. The Pack had scraped up just one division title since Lombardi's final season in '67, and the perception in Wisconsin was that only the great Bart Starr could restore his team to glory.

"I wasn't ready to be a coach," Starr conceded long afterwards. "I didn't have the experience and we didn't have the kind of solid, veteran team where you could win and learn as you went. It was difficult."

And then some.

Starr lasted nine years in the job, fighting to rebuild the Packers, and felt he'd become a pretty decent coach by the time he was dismissed following the 1983 season. So the whole situation became very unpleasant — fans at last grumbling about their once-untouchable icon and the club's executive committee feeling pressured to move in another direction.

"It wasn't the happiest time," Starr said, "but nothing can change my feelings or my loyalty to the Packers. I'll always be Green Bay's biggest fan. I'll be excited all over again when the Packers get back to the Super Bowl."

Whatever dent the coaching letdown might have put in Starr's almost

After his first few years in the NFL, no one ever questioned Starr's leadership or play-calling. He was a master running the Packer attack — whether finding the right spot for a give to Paul Hornung (5) or surveying the defense to exploit a weak spot.

Bart Starr: He'll always be remembered as Mr. Quarterback in Green Bay.

Incredibly popular with the fans in Green Bay, Starr received a true hero's ovation during a special ceremony for him at Lambeau Field.

Olympian reputation, he remains a quarterback for the ages — triggerman on some of the best teams Green Bay or any other franchise will ever see.

All-Pro guard Jerry Kramer summed up Starr's tenure this way: "Bart was rarely the best quarterback in the league on a statistical basis. But for three hours each Sunday, he was — almost always — the best quarterback in the game in which he was playing.

". . . Bart always said the right thing, always did the right thing. All the years (11) we played together, I looked for a flaw, waited for a slip, an inconsistency, a contradiction in his nature. I never spotted one."

As Kramer and others have said over and over while reminiscing about the giddy success of the 1960s, Bart Starr often seemed too good to be true.

He was good. And he *was* true.

But if you're fervently searching for some sort of manly truth in football's violent cauldron, look no further than Starr's longtime teammate, the Packers' relentless, snorting, snarling No. 66 — middle linebacker Ray Nitschke.

As different as the rough-and-tumble, hard-boiled Nitschke might have been from Starr in terms of personality and comportment — both on and off the field — these two Hall of Famers had some telling things in common.

They both preceded Lombardi to Green Bay, for one thing, and each man was a frustrated, chafing bench-warmer who took some time convincing the new coach that he should be out there every play — winning games and championships — instead of watching from the sidelines. Like Starr, Nitschke had to bide his time in 1959, Lombardi's first season, until the coach had sorted out exactly who were his winners and what other players weren't.

Unlike Bart, though, the outspoken Nitschke made his frustration apparent. The former fullback-linebacker from Illinois wanted to be playing every down, hitting people, when Lombardi thought he should be learning from a distance.

Which brings up the Nitschke credo.

"I've always thought I was the best middle linebacker in professional football," he said. "And not just because the National Football League picked me as the top man at that job in the league's first fifty years.

"I thought I was the best middle linebacker even when I was a rookie, trying to beat my good friend, Tom Bettis, out of a starting job. I thought so (in 1971) even when I sat on the bench after Coach Dan Devine gave Jim Carter my job.

"Whenever I went onto the field, I was the best middle linebacker. I had to be. Otherwise, it wouldn't have been fair, because the center who was trying to block me thought he was the best center who ever lived, and that back who was trying to get past me with the ball thought he was the best halfback or fullback created since the game began.

"When that back with the ball was coming at me, he was telling himself, 'Nobody's going to stop me before I get a touchdown because I'm the best damned runner in the world.'

"If I didn't think I was the best middle linebacker, how would I stop him?

"And if I'm out there, I'm going to stop him. I'm going to hit him. I'm going to let him know I'm still around. I don't intend that he'll make an inch, let alone a touchdown, and then I want him to go back to the huddle shaking his head and thinking about Ray Nitschke. I want him to remember Ray Nitschke, even in his dreams."

Most of 'em did.

Nitschke wasn't fancy, wasn't blessed with the eye-popping size or speed that you see with some of today's carved-from-stone linebackers. He was simply a hitter, a pursuer, an unstoppable dealer of punishment. And most of all, he was a tackler. In fact, Nitschke was the guy who totally took to heart Lombardi's favorite description of tackling.

"If a man is running down the street with everything you own, you won't let him get away," Lombardi said. "That's tackling."

Nitschke played it just that way, as though every ballcarrier, every pass receiver, had just robbed his house and was hustling away with his life's wealth. He took it personally.

And he was tough. Lord, he was tough.

In a rock-and-sock career that spanned the seasons from 1958–72, Nitschke played and hit through injuries, heat, cold — he suffered frostbite in the Ice Bowl game of '67 — and whatever else stood in his way. He seemed indestructible.

The best tale to illustrate how the Packers — and certainly their opponents — looked at Nitschke concerned a practice-field incident.

A fierce rainstorm was looming one afternoon and, rather than get drenched in the next moment or two, Nitschke had hustled underneath a huge steel observation tower — the one coaches and film crews use to watch workouts. But then a furious wind caught the structure and knocked it over — right onto Nitschke.

Play stopped and everyone gawked, terrified to see that somebody had been crushed under the tower.

Lombardi must have been near panic. "Who is it? Who got hit?" he said. Told that it was Nitschke, Lombardi let out a deep breath and turned away to resume practice.

"He knew nothing could hurt my head," Nitschke joked, although it really had been a close call — a bolt from the tower actually pierced his helmet and just missed inflicting horrendous damage.

Also like Starr, Nitschke always seemed to find another level of play in the biggest games. He was the emotional leader of the defense as Starr was on offense. And like Lombardi, Nitschke looked upon losing as something like an insult against his manhood.

The NFL championship game following the 1965 season might have showcased Nitschke's finest performance. He was assigned to shadow Jim Brown, Cleveland's all-world running back, and somehow contain a man who had run past, over and through everyone in his path since he'd first set foot in the league.

Lombardi was thinking of Brown when he posted a sign in the locker room that read: "Pursuit is the shortest course to the ballcarrier and arriving there in bad humor."

Nitschke claims he told himself: "Brown's your responsibility. Here's a big challenge. Are you big enough to handle it? Are you a big enough

Could anyone possibly as tough as Ray Nitschke, the Packers' Hall of Fame middle linebacker? Nitschke was the rock around which Green Bay's championship defenses were built.

(Above) The sight of Nitschke struck terror into the hearts of ballcarriers, and he wanted it that way. Nitschke often said he wanted offensive backs to have dreams about him — not necessarily pleasant ones, either.

(Right) The Big Three: Linebackers Dave Robinson (left), Nitschke and Lee Roy Caffey discuss things on the sideline.

Intense, relentless, angry in pursuit and always ready to hit: Ray Nitscke was rightfully voted the best middle linebacker in the NFL's first 50 years.

man to stop him? You're big enough and strong enough, but can you do it?"

He did it.

Brown was held to 50 yards on 12 carries — and dropped an apparent touchdown pass — as the Packers won 23–12 to reclaim the league title after a two-year drought.

"You know that pass Brown dropped in the end zone?" offensive tackle Bob Skoronski said. "He had it in his hands but Nitschke was all over him, just hustling and hollering and screaming at him."

Even Brown grudgingly paid his respects.

"I noticed that Ray Nitschke was keying on me," Brown said. "He's as tough as anybody is."

What a perfect way to sum up Nitschke's career: He was as tough as anybody.

The other two Packers whose numbers have been retired pre-dated the Lombardi era: Don Hutson and Tony Canadeo. But that pair did have something in common with the big-name stars of the 1960s: Both played on teams that won NFL championships — Hutson in 1936 and '39, Canadeo in 1944.

Hutson was almost a revolutionary in the sense that he turned pass-receiving into an art form — not to mention a frightening offensive weapon — at a time when most pro teams still believed you could only win championships by running the football.

The numbers are staggering for any age, but considering that Hutson arrived in the NFL in 1935 when passing games were still terribly unsophisticated, some of his records boggle the mind.

How about 99 touchdown catches in 11 seasons? By current standards, that seems more like 200. Those 99 scoring receptions weren't matched for nearly a half-century.

Hutson caught 488 throws for 7,991 yards in his career, despite being covered by everyone except the other team's water boy. And remember, those were the days of drastically shorter schedules.

You can make the case that no one player ever dominated pro football for a decade the way Hutson did from 1935–45, which is saying something since Hutson was a scrawny-looking 6-footer who worked to keep his weight somewhere around 175 pounds.

He didn't appear to be a blazer, either, although opponents often discovered to their chagrin that Hutson was an outstanding athlete with several changes of speed, a deceptive gait that made him appear to be running at half speed when he had plenty left — and tremendous leaping ability. He also had large, powerful hands that always seemed to be clutching the football when it came down in a crowd.

That was the era of one-platoon players, too, and Hutson probably could have been a Hall of Famer playing defense alone. He once led the league in interceptions, using all those same uncanny skills and a knack for finding the ball that rarely has been matched in the NFL.

Could Hutson have been so dominant in another era?

Most football people think so, including Canadeo, who played with Hutson from 1940 to '44.

"He was the best athlete I played with or against," Canadeo said. "He was a gifted receiver and a great defensive player. He could play in today's league and be a star. He had all the moves, the speed, the hands. He caught the ball in those years, and he could have caught them in *any* years."

Hutson's sensational debut against the Bears in 1935 already has been mentioned, but actually he turned in two performances that season against Green Bay's fiercest rival that truly introduced this pass-catching legend to pro football.

First came the bomb at home in the '35 opener, when the Packers began the season at their own 16-yard line and debuted a star just one play later. Quarterback Arnie Herber dropped into his own end zone and simply heaved a monstrous pass — as far as he could throw one.

Bears Hall of Fame safety Beattie Feathers remembered it long afterward.

"I saw Herber throw this pass downfield," Feathers said, "and this lanky guy loping down toward me. I knew the ball was going way over my head, and I was sure it was way out of Hutson's reach. But all of a sudden, he turned on his speed, ran right by me, took the pass in perfect stride and went on for a touchdown."

The Packers won that game 7–0, but Hutson was even more spectacular when the two teams met again in Chicago.

Green Bay trailed 14–3 with barely three minutes remaining, when Hutson caught a pass in the flat and somehow eluded what seemed to be the entire Bear team en route to the goal line. He'd cut the deficit to 14–10 but only about a minute was left.

When the Bears got the ball back, Green Bay tackle Ernie Smith put a fierce hit on fullback Bronko Nagurski, forced a fumble and fell on it.

On the next play, Hutson worked his way clear in the deep corner of the end zone and snared Herber's desperation pass just inches inside the field of play. The Packers won 17–14 and Hutson's arrival was official.

There was another aspect to Hutson's heroic career, as well. He performed his magic just when the franchise needed him most — in a time of financial struggles when the very existence of pro football in Green Bay was hanging by a thread.

Perhaps no one dominated the league for a decade as Don Hutson did from the mid-1930s to the middle '40s. Hutson posed with nine footballs, one for each NFL record he held in 1943.

Wide open again: Hutson often blew right past defenders to haul in touchdown passes. He caught a league-record 99 TD throws.

Hutson remained a legend long after his playing career. He was asked to toss the ceremonial coin at midfield prior to Super Bowl XXII in San Diego.

Tony Canadeo, the Grey Ghost of Gonzaga, was elected to the Pro Football Hall of Fame on the strength of overall brilliance — whether he was running the ball on offense or preparing to make a jarring tackle in the defensive secondary.

Canadeo (3) wasn't the type of player to let conditions slow him down. He was as happy to put his nose toward the goal line in a snowstorm as he was in sunshine.

Tony Canadeo has been part of the Packer family for a half-century — as a star player, broadcaster and then as a longtime member of franchise board of directors.

In every possible way, Hutson was a star of stars.

And what about Canadeo, whose career overlapped Hutson's in that same era of fiscal uncertainly?

They called him the Grey Ghost of Gonzaga — referring to his alma mater and a premature thatch of silvery hair — but Canadeo was hardly a will-o-the-wisp running back.

"I wasn't very tall and I played at about 190 pounds," Canadeo said. "My game was to hit the hole as quick as I could and keep going forward. Nothing fancy, just hit the hole and go.

"Maybe that's the Green Bay mentality: Always go straight for the goal line."

Canadeo's contributions to the Packer organization are both amazing and enduring. He became just the third man in NFL history to rush for 1,000 yards when he rang up 1,052 in 1949, and he scored 31 touchdowns despite missing most of 1944 and all of the '45 season because of World War II.

"I would loved to have had those two full seasons," he said. "That's when I was 25 and 26 years old and playing my best. And we won the championship in 1944."

Canadeo only managed a cameo role in that title year, carrying the ball just 31 times.

Perhaps the Grey Ghost's most lasting efforts, though, came after his playing career ended in 1952. He stayed on in Green Bay as one of the club's radio broadcasters and then was elected to the Packers board of directors in 1955. Canadeo became a member of the executive committee in 1958 and served with distinction — often helping make crucial decisions on football matters — until stepping down on his 74th birthday in 1993.

Nobody — not even Lambeau — has been with the Packers longer than Tony Canadeo.

So those are the only four men whose numbers have been retired in Green Bay. But another earned the honor on a temporary basis.

Paul Hornung's famous No. 5 has been re-issued since his departure from pro football — quarterback Don Majkowski even started with it before switching to No. 7 in deference to Hornung — but for awhile, it was considered untouchable.

Why? Because Vince Lombardi said so.

It was Lombardi who turned Hornung into an all-purpose superstar, Lombardi who first realized Paul's remarkable ability to outdo himself close to the end zone — and Lombardi who became almost physically ill when the New Orleans Saints chose the injured Hornung in the 1967 expansion draft.

"No one else will wear Paul Hornung's number as long as I'm in Green Bay," Lombardi said.

Hornung surely deserved the accolade, since he represented — more than any other single player — Green Bay's ascent to dominance in the early 1960s.

Forget the career numbers, though they're impressive. Sure, Hornung scored 62 touchdowns, converted 190 points after touchdowns and kicked 66 field goals for a total of 760 points. All that despite missing the '63 season while he was suspended for gambling. He led the league in scoring from 1959–61 and once scored 19 points in a championship-game victory.

What really separated Hornung from everyone else was his versatility, his incredible nose for the goal line and, yes, his flamboyant personality. The Golden Boy from Notre Dame was king of the nightlife, a free spirit who brought sheer excitement to the Packers inside the white lines and out.

Lombardi loved him, pure and simple.

"You know, I always wondered myself why he liked me so much," Hornung said. "I think that vicariously he would have liked to have been in my position — you know, the good life, a bachelor and all. Maybe. I don't know."

What everyone *did* know was that fun-loving characters like Hornung and his free-wheeling pal Max McGee somehow appealed to Lombardi — even as the coach instilled thunderous discipline on his championship teams.

Hornung was late getting on the team bus one day — a huge no-no in Lombardi's book — and when he walked past the coach, Lombardi roared: "Where have you been?"

Everyone was terrified what might happen, but Hornung blithely replied, "I've been to church," and kept right on striding toward the back of the bus.

Lombardi exploded with laughter. "Church!" he cried. "How do you like that? He's been to church."

Hornung was a lot more than just the team comedian, though. He'd been a bonus draft pick in 1957 after winning the Heisman Trophy as a quarterback. Green Bay's coaches before Lombardi tried Hornung at that spot but he wasn't a great pure passer.

What Lombardi spotted was Hornung's amazing variety of skills. He was a tough, hard-nosed runner, a vicious blocker and, obviously, once moved to halfback he became a dangerous weapon anytime the Packers wanted to use an option pass. But beyond that was Hornung's uncanny ability to score.

"No matter what happens out in the middle of the field," Lombardi said, "it's different when we have a chance to score. When you get down near the goal line, Paul Hornung is the toughest guy I've ever seen. The toughest."

It's no accident that so many Packer greats played in the Lombardi era. There were stars in the early years — after all, Green Bay won six world championships before anyone in Wisconsin had ever heard of Vince Lombardi — and some talented athletes have come along since.

And lest anyone get caught up solely in the glory years alone, the Packers showcased some genuine stars even in those down cycles when won-lost records fell far below the usual Green Bay standards. In the best-be-forgotten 1950s — which produced nary a winning season until Lombardi's arrival in '59 — men like quarterback Tobin Rote, receiver Bill Howton and defensive back Bobby Dillon were just about as good as anyone in the league at their positions.

In the sometimes-frustrating post-Lombardi years, more exciting players emerged: Bomb-throwing Lynn Dickey, iron-man center Larry

Paul Hornung, the Golden Boy, took Green Bay by storm when he arrived from Notre Dame in the late 1950s. In just a few years, he and offensive tackle Bob Skoronski (76) were helping execute an offense that dominated the NFL.

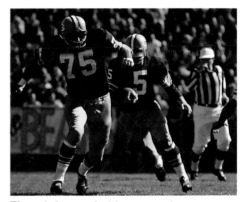

Though he made his reputation as a triple-threat player who could damage defenses in all sorts of ways, Hornung was a heady runner who could find the hole. That's Hall of Fame tackle Forrest Gregg (75) leading the charge.

Hornung (left) on the bench with a couple of his pals and running mates, Max McGee (center) and Jim Taylor.

Vince Lombardi called Hornung the greatest player he ever saw when his team got close to the goal line. Here he dives over to score against San Francisco.

On guard: The three offensive guards who spearheaded the famous Packer sweeps talk it over — Jerry Kramer (left), Fuzzy Thurston (center) and Gale Gillingham.

Jim Taylor was one of the toughest runners ever to play pro football. He loved to explode through an opening, like the one provided by guard Fuzzy Thurston (63), and then begin mowing down tacklers in the secondary.

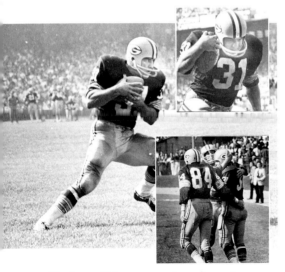

Taylor will be remembered most as a runner, but he could catch the ball and make things happen, as he did on scoring pass against Cleveland. That's wide receiver Carrol Dale (84) joining the end zone celebration.

McCarren, defensive back Willie Buchanon and that breathtaking duo on the flanks, James Lofton and John Jefferson — among others.

That doesn't even take into account some current stars, who are almost certain to rank someday among Packer greats.

But the Lombardi era brought a bonanza of talent. He seemed able to stockpile outstanding players. Lombardi inherited some and acquired a few more who had sensational natural skills, but he also molded or reinvented several others who once had seemed capable of only limited success. Willie Wood went undrafted out of college, Herb Adderley was a converted running back and Cleveland traded away Willie Davis.

Hornung's backfield partner, Jim Taylor, represented the classic case.

Until Lombardi arrived, the word on Taylor was that he was too slow a learner to be dependable in any offense. Hard as nails, certainly, and as ruthless a ballcarrier as you'd ever need, but possibly not savvy enough to be an everyday contributor.

Lombardi decided immediately that he wasn't trying to teach anyone rocket science. He wanted yardage and touchdowns, and Taylor could provide them. In Lombardi's "Run to Daylight" scheme, Taylor became a fearful battering ram. He exploded past the line of scrimmage and then sought out potential tacklers, intending to inflict as much damage as he could.

There was nothing fancy about Jim Taylor. He was pure power.

After Lombardi left Green Bay to coach the Washington Redskins, he was showing his new team some Packer films — he was trying to install a similar offense. The coach found one particular clip of Taylor trampling people and ran the film over and over. He seemed transfixed by it.

Finally, Lombardi said, "Would you just look at that son of a bitch run?"

Recall what Tony Canadeo said about the Green Bay mentality — straight for the goal line. That was the trademark of almost all the Packer greats from any era. This franchise hasn't produced many Fred Astaire types — no hot-footers or swivel-hip dancers. In Green Bay, it's been the

Willie Wood, shown conferring with defensive coordinator Phil Bengtson, was the emotional leader of the Packers secondary during those championship years in the 1960s.

Wood (24) had been an undrafted free agent coming out of college, but by the time he joined the Packers, he'd learned to combine toughness with pure athletic skills.

no-nonsense, bust-your-butt guys who have succeeded — and that includes the superstars.

Many of Lombardi's best players were foot soldiers — linemen Gregg, Davis, Skoronski, Henry Jordan and that remarkable pair of guards, Kramer and Thurston. Even the great pure athletes, like defensive backs Wood and Adderley or receivers Boyd Dowler and McGee, were rock tough in addition to everything else.

Almost no one ever frightened Ray Nitschke, but he enjoys talking about the intensity of Wood, the Hall of Fame safety who played behind him. "I always hated the thought of missing a tackle," Nitschke said. "It was bad enough to let a runner get away, but I was scared of the way Willie would stare at me. He had a look that was unbelievable."

An interesting postscript to those glory days was that Lombardi singled out Gregg, an offensive lineman and later a Packer coach himself, as the best football player he ever coached.

Kramer apparently agreed.

In his book about a Packer reunion in 1984, Kramer wrote of Gregg: "Forrest, at right tackle, and I played next to each other for most of 11 seasons. In 1964, when I was hospitalized for internal bleeding that sparked rumors I was dying of cancer, Forrest moved into my position and made all-pro at both guard and tackle.

"Forrest was big, but he didn't overpower opponents. He was a master of technique, of position. He would shield, slide, maneuver and almost always get the job done. . . . Forrest was a hell of a player, a hell of a person."

Any mention of Kramer brings up one of the great injustices ever done in handing out accolades for career accomplishments. Even though he was voted the best offensive guard in the NFL's first 50 years, Kramer somehow has missed being elected to the Pro Football Hall of Fame.

There is no excuse, obviously. But a reason? It's probably the fact that so many players from Lombardi's teams already have been enshrined at Canton. Nonetheless, Jerry Kramer's name belongs on that list of greats — not only in Green Bay, but in the Hall itself.

If he's eventually given the spot at Canton he deserves, Kramer surely

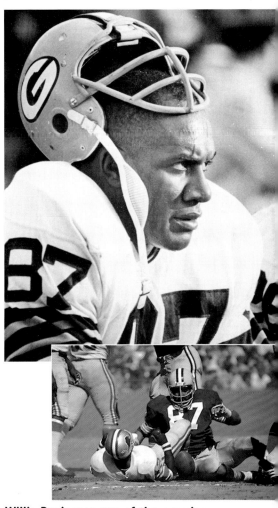

Willie Davis was one of the premier defensive ends in NFL history, a one-time castoff who became the Packers' defensive captain and eventually a Hall of Fame player.

Wherever Davis went, sacks and sometimes fumbles — like this one against the Lions — were almost sure to happen.

All in a day's work: Defensive backfield stars Herb Adderley (26), Bob Jeter (22) and Willie Wood leave the field after turning away yet another foe.

(Left) Herb Adderley was a college star as a runner, but he became a Hall of Fame cornerback with the Packers.

Defensive tackle Henry Jordan (74) was one of the quickest players at the line of scrimmage ever to play for the Packers.

Even the Packers' best athletes had to be tough. That's receiver Boyd Dowler (86) wrestling loose to snare a third-down pass.

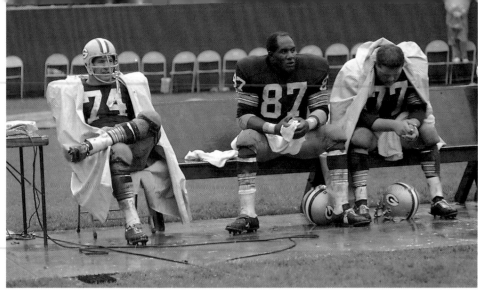

Defensive linemen Henry Jordan (left), Willie Davis (center) and Ron Kostelnik take a rest after a goal-line stand. All three played key roles on the Lombardi-era teams.

will have plenty of company from other Packers. In addition to the 18 Hall of Famers who spent the bulk of their time in Green Bay, four more Packers — Walt Kiesling, Emlen Tunnell, Ted Hendricks and Jan Stenerud — already have been inducted.

It's an impressive list, and it started early. Some of those Packer greats who now are remembered only through granddad's stories or fuzzy black-and-white photographs were larger-than-life heroes who could have been dominant players in any decade.

Almost certainly the most exciting was McNally, the kid who changed his name to Blood but never altered his devil-may-care attitude — and whose multiple skills won games and titles for the Lambeau teams.

Here was Hornung's natural predecessor. Johnny Blood actually jumped a freight train — actually, two trains — just finding his way to Green Bay in the first place. Typically, he charmed one railroad crewman to the point that the man not only let him ride illegally, he offered Johnny his lunch.

Blood was no stranger to bottled spirits; in fact, he was a non-stop partier who once showed up at practice in New York — this was the day before a critical game against the Giants — in such bad shape that he fell flat on his backside trying to punt the ball. The frustrated Lambeau had to be talked out of cutting his star on the spot, just as Curly later caved in when Blood missed the start of the 1936 season as the Packers' first-ever contract holdout.

Lambeau did his best to keep Blood under some sort of control, even rooming him with another, far more responsible Hall of Famer, tackler Mike Michalske. That didn't work, either — which was just about Michalske's only failure in a magnificent career that ran from 1929–37 and included four championships.

Although Michalske was a rugged, talented player, he barely weighed 200 pounds. A couple of other Packer brutes from the early days — Cub Buck and Cal Hubbard — were far bigger. Matter of fact, they were considered giants at the time and each was an overwhelming presence in the years he played.

Packers in the
Pro Football Hall of Fame

1963 — E.L. "Curly" Lambeau
Founder, player, coach, vice president (1919–49)

Gary Thomas

1963 — Johnny (Blood) McNally
Halfback (1928–36)

1963 — Don Hutson
End (1935–45)

1963 — Johnny (Blood) McNally
Halfback (1928–36)

1964 — Clarke Hinkle
Fullback (1932–41)

1963 — Robert "Cal" Hubbard
Tackle (1929–35)

1963 — Don Hutson
End (1935–45)

1971 — Vince Lombardi
Coach and General Manager (1959-67)

1977 — Forrest Gregg
Tackle (1956, 1958–70)

1971 — Vince Lombardi
Coach and General Manager (1959–67)

1966 — Arnie Herber
Quarterback (1930–41)

1964 — Mike Michalske
Guard (1929–37)

1974 — Tony Canadeo
Halfback (1941–44, 1946–52)

1976 — Jim Taylor
Fullback (1958–66)

1977 — Forrest Gregg
Tackle (1956, 1958–70)

Bart Starr
Quarterback (1956–71)

1978 — Ray Nitschke
Middle Linebacker (1958–72)

1980 — Herb Adderley
Defensive Back (1961–69)

1981 — Jim Ringo
Center (1953–63)

1981 — Willie Davis
Defensive End (1960–69)

Gary Thomas

1986 — Paul Hornung
Halfback (1957–62, 1964–

Gary Thomas

1989 — Willie Wood
Free Safety (1960 - 71)

Gary Thomas

Forrest Gregg made all-pro both at guard and tackle, and Lombardi paid him the ultimate compliment when he said Gregg was the best football player he ever coached.

(Left) A sensational running back and kicker, Ted Fritsch (64) scored 380 points in a Green Bay career that spanned the years 1942–50. He once kicked a 52-yard field goal, a monstrous boot for that era.

(Right) Among the Packers' early stars, guard Mike Michalske was a standout, though this future Hall of Famer weighed only 200 pounds.

Long after his playing career was over, quarterback Arnie Herber remained a favorite with Green Bay fans. Herber was considered one of the most accurate passers in NFL history.

(Opposite page) During the glory days of the Lombardi era, quarterback Bart Starr was always the man in charge on the field.

A couple of Packer legends, Clarke Hinkle (30) and Don Hutson (14), prepare to do some damage to a ballcarrier. Hinkle and Hutson were two-way stars who got head-lines on offense but also helped win championships with outstanding defensive play.

And speaking of dominating, the Packers later landed one of the roughest customers the game has ever seen, fullback Clarke Hinkle.

Lambeau, who was an outright genius at finding, acquiring and moving talent according to what he needed at the time, turned over almost the entire roster in the years immediately after his triple championships of 1929–31. Hutson came along in '35, of course, but despite what anyone said, he wasn't exactly a one-man team.

The Packers' title teams of the 1930s surely couldn't have won without Hinkle or quarterback Arnie Herber, among others. Hinkle, a powerful fullback from Bucknell College, gave Green Bay a perfect counterpoint to Bronko Nagurski, the Bears' awesome two-way bruiser. And as usual, the Bears were the team the Packers generally had to beat if they were thinking about championships.

The first meeting between Hinkle and Nagurski remains the stuff of legend. Hinkle was fine kicker — he booted 28 field goals — and in the second game of the season in 1932, he opened the game by kicking off to Nagurski. The result was a frightening collision at the Chicago 30-yard line. Both Hinkle and Nagurski were flattened, but Hinkle eventually managed to walk away while the great Bronko had to be carried off.

Herber, who played from 1930–41, may have been one of the most accurate passers of all time. In tandem with Hutson, he gave the Packers a frightening passing game that kept opponents continually on their heels.

A story worth retelling: During a Packers barnstorming tour to California, a company specializing in sports features decided to make a movie that included a segment on Herber's passing touch.

The hook was that a piece of plate glass would be hung from the goal post, and Herber was supposed to fire footballs at it — with cameras rolling — until he could shatter the thing. Don't worry, the producers told Herber, they had plenty of film and they'd keep shooting until he connected.

"What would you do that for?" Herber replied.

At which point, the Packer quarterback set himself 60 yards away, let fly and smashed the glass into a zillion pieces on his first attempt.

Whoever said there's no feel for show business in Green Bay? The Packers certainly have had enough stars for it. ❖

The Long Road Back

"When the Cowboys won the Super Bowl, Dallas went crazy. But when the Green Bay Packers win the Super Bowl again, all America will go crazy."

— Brett Favre

It's very likely that every man, woman and child who lives and dies with the fortunes of the Green Bay Packers is up, up, up these days.

You'd have trouble finding a Packer loyalist anywhere who doesn't believe that all the frustration, all the wheel-spinning of the past two decades has become ancient history; in fact, that the new-look Packers may be heading back toward another glory era.

The only thing that's tough to pinpoint — and a sampling of fans surely would produce different answers — is the exact moment when this proud franchise made the move, pulled off the trade or won the game to prove once and for all that the Pack not only is back, but rising like a river at flood stage.

Perhaps it happened with the elevation of Bob Harlan to president — he's been called Green Bay's renaissance man for good reason.

"We're coming off a very strong year, financially," Harlan said in a newspaper interview early in 1993. "We've always said we make our money in football and we spend our money in football.

"It doesn't do us a lot of good to pile up a big reserve. We want to take the money we make and either put it back in the facilities or put it into players and improve out football team.

"I'd hope everyone in the league would look at Green Bay now with some respect. It bothers me a great deal to think anybody looks down on Green Bay. The little city. This is too proud a franchise to be looked at like that.

The biggest off-season news the Packers have made in years occured after the 1992 season when free agent defensive end Reggie White spurned dozens of other offers to sign with Green Bay. White's arrival only heightened the fans' optimistic frenzy.

The man in charge: General Manager Ron Wolf was put in complete command of football operations in November of 1991 and, so far, he's made all the right moves.

"I'd hope that people say, 'Green Bay has some very capable people in that football operation. They're spending some money. They want to win. They're doing whatever it takes to build a winner.'"

Yes, people are saying that — because of some of the things Harlan and the Packers executive committee have done since taking over the reins.

Or maybe the magic point in time occurred when Harlan decided once and for all to put the team's football operations into the hands of a single individual — a proven winner at creating competitive teams — and hired general manager Ron Wolf.

Following that was Wolf's rapid-fire decision to relieve coach Lindy Infante — with three years left to be paid on his contract — after a disappointing 1991 season. Wolf turned right around and replaced Infante with Mike Holmgren, one of the architects of San Francisco's Super Bowl triumphs, and that hiring so far looks like an acquisition of sheer brilliance.

Linebacker Tony Bennett already has developed into one of the NFL's pass-rushing stars, and the Packers hope his best years are still ahead.

(Left) Record-setting wide receiver Sterling Sharpe is one of the most dangerous offensive weapons in the league. Now the Packers are finding other pass-catchers to complement Sharpe's skills and make the entire group even more productuve.

Or how about Wolf's first huge trade — albeit a controversial deal at the time? The new GM didn't hesitate to unload a first-round draft choice to Atlanta for backup quarterback Brett Favre, even though Wolf already had Don Majkowksi, a QB with some exciting things on his résumé.

It's been almost forgotten now, but Favre was something of an unknown commodity — at least to everyone but Wolf, who remembered this tough and hard-throwing leader from his junior season in college at Southern Mississippi. Favre was injured in a car accident prior to his senior year and, following serious surgery for internal injuries, his production fell off.

And then, of course, Favre had hardly played at all as a rookie at Atlanta in 1991. So eyebrows shot up when Wolf shipped off that precious draft choice to snag him.

How does the trade look now? You'd be hard pressed finding a soul around the NFL who doesn't believe that — barring injury or some other unforeseen setback — Favre won't develop into one of the league's marquee stars.

So now, is the search for precious turning point coming any closer?

Consider this: There may even have been some doubters, some skeptical folk who fretted that the oh-so-close brush with the playoffs in 1992 looked like a one-shot deal. If so, those last few doubters probably began hailing the Packers' complete resurrection when the club went out and signed a host of big-time free agents — most notably future Hall of Fame defensive end Reggie White.

Packer people tend to remember things that happen on the field, though, rather than paper transactions or shuffling in the front office.

And so you'd have to guess that most fans believe the Packers took the critical fork in their long road back to Super Bowl contention on September 20, 1992.

Fair enough. Who can forget that watershed afternoon at Lambeau Field?

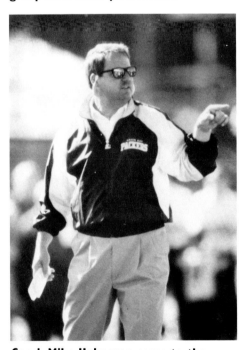

Coach Mike Holmgren came to the Packers with a fondness for winning. He'd helped San Francisco capture Super Bowl rings as offensive coach and coordinator.

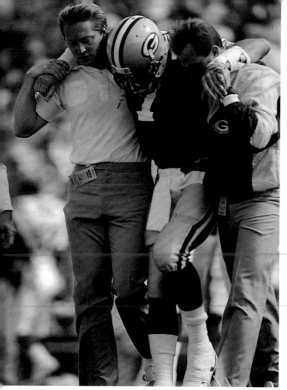

The entire future of Packer football changed in the third game of the 1992 season when incumbent quarterback Don Majkowski (above) hurt his ankle and precocious newcomer Brett Favre (opposite page) not only took over, but led Green Bay to a last-second victory over Cincinnati.

Ready to win: Veteran linebacker Brian Noble suffered through some tough years, but he's stuck around to see the Packers' fortunes improve.

The Packers had opened the year 0–2 as they struggled to grasp the new systems installed by rookie coach Holmgren and his staff. And then they trailed Cincinnati 17–3 early in the fourth quarter, setting up what seemed almost surely to be Green Bay's first 0–3 start since 1988. On top of everything else, Majkowski was gone, having had his left ankle smashed when he was sacked by Tim Krumrie back in the first quarter.

Enter Favre.

It wasn't exactly like the untested gunslinger lit it up from the beginning, either.

"I was shaking," Favre said of his entrance as Majkowski's successor — at a time when he clearly was baffled by some aspects of Holmgren's complicated offense. "I felt like I took a laxative. Thank God I held it until the end."

Through most of the game, Favre occasionally did look lost.

"We got into some of the darnedest formations I've ever seen," Holmgren said. "But we started to settle down and good things started to happen."

Great things, actually.

Favre went on to complete 22 of 39 passes in his Green Bay debut, but the big ones came late. And the monster arrived latest of all.

Another first-year player, Florida State rookie Terrell Buckley, gave a hint of the heroics to follow when he returned a punt 58 yards for a touchdown with 12:43 left to play, cutting Cincinnati's once-comfortable lead to 17–10.

The Bengals responded with a drive for a field goal and 20–10, but Favre was discovering ever-growing confidence, and he swept the Packers downfield on an eight-play, 88-yard drive that finished with a 5-yard touchdown pass to the incomparable Sterling Sharpe.

Cincinnati added another field goal after a Buckley fumble, and bumped up the margin again when kicker Jim Breech made a 41-yarder with 1:07 remaining — leaving Favre and the Packers down 23–17 and needing a miracle.

They got it.

Favre and Co. zoomed up unfield despite starting at their own 8-yard line. A 42-yard throw to Sharpe brought the end zone into reasonable heaving distance and, with 19 seconds remaining at Cincinnati 35, that's what the gutty Favre decided to do. Sling it and hope.

"It was four guys going deep," Favre said. "That last ball, I was scared I was going to throw it halfway up the stands. I just closed my eyes and waited for the cheering."

Which wasn't long in coming, since Favre's bullet found Kitrick Taylor roaring into the right corner of the end zone — and the Packers had officially leaped into the Holmgren era with a 24–23 victory.

That incredible comeback produced all sorts of wonderful side effects. It sent a shock wave of bravado through a young team fighting to find its own identity, and it established beyond a doubt that Favre — however meager the experience he brought to the party — was something very, very special.

"What you see in Brett is a young guy who loves to play," Holmgren

He may be outspoken — sometimes ridiculously so — but second-year cornerback Terrell Buckley gives the Packers speed, breathtaking athletic ability and sheer excitement.

Happiness is finding outstanding defensive help in the college draft, and the Packers believe they did it in 1993 by picking linebacker Wayne Simmons and defensive back George Teague with their first two choices.

When the long, tough climb back really began — Phil Bengtson had been a brilliant defensive coordinator for Vince Lombardi, but things went wrong immediately when he was thrust into the limelight as head coach from 1968–70.

said. "He'll drive you a little nuts some of the time and he'll make big play some of the time. But he's a player. He certainly makes my life interesting."

And more enjoyable.

Favre eventually led the Packers to a 9–7 record that was better than it looked, considering the circumstances. And he wound up in the Pro Bowl — which was a long way from sitting on the bench in Atlanta, or even Green Bay.

Several other Packers had outstanding individual seasons that either marked them for stardom or merely confirmed it.

Linebacker Tony Bennett, who is rapidly becoming a force throughout the NFL, recorded 13.5 sacks, forced 4 fumbles and recovered 3 more bobbles — including an 18-yard return for a touchdown.

Placekicker Chris Jacke converted all 30 of his PAT attempts, running his current streak to 86, and hit on a very efficient 22 of 29 field goals.

And then there was Sharpe, who stamped himself again — along with San Francisco's Jerry Rice — as one of the game's show-stopping receivers. Sharpe set an NFL record with 108 catches, breaking Art Monk's previous mark of 106.

But that was only part of the story. Even without a true deep threat on the other side to lure defenders away from him, Sharpe became the first Packer since Don Hutson in 1944 to lead the league in catches, yards (1,461) and touchdowns (13).

Just how good is Sterling Sharpe?

"If we give him some help and find other people who can get open and catch the ball consistently, Sterling probably will rewrite all his own records," Holmgren said. "I'm a big fan of Jerry Rice and I coached him in San Francisco, but I'm not sure Sterling has to step back for anybody."

Speaking of finding help to free up Sharpe, the Packers not only signed longtime Miami deep threat Mark Clayton, but they're fully confident that tight end Jackie Harris (55 catches in '92) is a blooming superstar.

So now, with free agent acquisitions like White, Clayton, Tunch Ilkin, Bill Maas and Harry Galbreath in the mix — not to mention added defensive help from draft choices Wayne Simmons and George Teague — expectations in title-starved Packer country are almost out of sight.

"All of a sudden, people are talking about the Super Bowl," Wolf said. "I want to tell them, 'Whoa, we've got think about winning our own division. First things first.' But it's great that the enthusiasm is back. We'll never shy away from that. We want to return to a situation where the fans expect to win."

That sensation certainly has been a long time coming.

For a franchise steeped in championship tradition through dominance in the Lambeau and Lombardi eras, the Packers wallowed in mediocrity far longer than the faithful ever might have feared: two-plus decades, if anybody kept the stomach to count.

The decline started almost immediately after Vince Lombardi left the sidelines — having produced five titles in nine seasons — and became general manager following the 1967 season. Lombardi anointed super-sharp defensive coordinator Phil Bengtson as his heir apparent.

Dan Devine hardly got off to an auspicious start when he took over as coach in 1971. Devine broke his leg in a sideline collision and had to work on crutches.

(Left) The Packers had one season of success under Devine, winning the division championship in 1972 behind the bruising running of John Brockington (42) and MacArthur Lane (36).

Even with things going well in 1972, Devine had his problems — in particular lack of confidence in quarterback Scott Hunter.

The last of the old guard: Battered but not beaten center Ken Bowman — a holdover from the Lombardi days — anchored the Packers' running attack in '72.

Bengtson's lot following the legendary Lombardi would have been a rough one in any case, but just to make things even more difficult, several key players from that magnificent run in the 1960s either left football or were slipping well past their prime.

Those thunder-and-lightning running backs, Paul Hornung and Jim Taylor, each had departed earlier — after the Super Bowl I triumph in 1966. By the time Bengtson took over, quarterback Bart Starr had an ailing shoulder and quite a few other veterans were suffering an from accumulation of various hurts. But perhaps the most telling loss of all — at least in Bengtson's first year — was the retirement of veteran placekicker Don Chandler.

The Packers struggled to a 6–7–1 record in 1968, but five of those losses came by margins of a touchdown or less, and many were the direct result of kicking failures. Bengtson tried anybody who could swing a leg, it seemed, and the situation became so ludicrous that the Packers imported a kicking guru from nearby Appleton — a man with no NFL experience at any level.

That didn't help, either, and it signified the frustrations of Bengtson's three trying seasons as head coach. He coaxed an 8–6 record out of the '69 team, but then resigned after a 6–8 disappointment the following year.

By that time, almost everyone from the great teams was gone and a long, unpleasant slide had begun — though Green Bay partisans used to fairly regular success surely couldn't have guessed the extent of the decline.

The Packers' executive committee tried a new approach for 1971, importing a highly successful college coach, Dan Devine. That move appeared to offer a fresh start — and Devine did produce a single division championship in 1972 — but the more appropriate omen was

There were some thrilling newcomers in the Devine era, too, talented players like defensive back Willie Buchanon (28).

(Right) Dan Devine's tenure in Green Bay was marked by a trade that hurt the team for years. Devine dealt five draft choices to the Rams for aging quarterback John Hadl (center).

The people's choice: Local legend Bart Starr was a popular selection when the Packers brought him back as head coach in 1974.

Bombs away! Starr's teams created prolific offense, much of it from the arm of quarterback Lynn Dickey (12), who set up to let another one fly behind the blocking of iron-man center Larry McCarren.

delivered when Devine got clobbered on the sidelines and suffered a broken leg during his first regular-season game.

Devine's departure from Green Bay after four years was an unhappy one, and he left the cupboard bare with one disastrous trade, but the uptick in '72 is worth remembering — if for no other reason than that so few decent seasons loomed on the horizon.

The Packers that year appeared to have rediscovered an old, happy formula; which is to say, they ran the football with impunity. Devine installed an elephant backfield built around a couple of 220-pounders, John Brockington and MacArthur Lane, and turned the herd loose for 2,128 yards rushing.

"We flat-out ran over everybody," center Ken Bowman said. "Once you got those two (Brockington and Lane) in the backfield, it really didn't matter who you handed the ball to. We could move the ball on anybody."

Of course, part of the rationale for staying with an infantry attack was that no one — Devine included — had exceptional faith in journeyman quarterback Scott Hunter. In fact, Devine admitted later that he often admonished Hunter not to try anything silly with a forward pass when another three yards and a cloud of dust would do just fine.

"I remember we'd be leading late in a game and I'd call time out and bring Scott over to the sidelines," Devine said. "I'd tell him to take off his helmet and look me straight in the eye. Then I'd tell him: 'Scott, the only way we can lose this game is if you screw up.' Then I'd send him back to the huddle."

The giddiness of 1972 kind of snuck up on everyone. The Packers had a 4–8–2 record in Devine's first go-round the previous season, but there were solid additions through the draft — kicker Chester Marcol, defensive back Willie Buchanon and linebacker Dave Pureifory, among others. Lane had been acquired in a blockbuster trade with St. Louis for one of the last Lombardi-dynasty stars, Donny Anderson.

Neither rain, sleet nor snow could stop the Packer offense with Dickey throwing long and often, as the Pack proved by rolling up big yardage despite a Denver blizzard.

Devine also made another big move, which wasn't especially popular with the paying customers. He benched the aging Hall of Famer, Ray Nitschke, and installed Jim Carter at middle linebacker. Carter played well, but perhaps never well enough to win the hearts of fans who loved Nitschke.

Still, with all this surprising new help, the Packers went 10–4 — finishing the regular season with three straight victories to clinch the NFC Central Division title.

"It was a team that played over its head," Devine said, "but there were good players at every position. There weren't any bad weaknesses and we didn't luck out any games."

Well, even Devine himself knew there was at least one potential weakness with the steady but not particularly gifted Hunter at quarterback. That chink in the armor was exposed in the playoffs, when Washington used a five-man defensive front to stifle the Packers' running game and hammered out a 16–3 victory.

The Hunter Factor came into play again long after the unexpected bonanza of 1972, as well. When the Packers slipped to 5–7–2 in '73, Devine made a colossal blunder that eventually helped hasten his departure from Green Bay.

Searching for a proven quarterback, Devine obtained veteran John Hadl from the Rams — and paid a stupendous price. He gave up the

Hall of Fame kicker Jan Stenerud came to Green Bay in time for those offensive explosions of the early 1980s, and his accurate leg added to the scoring punch.

215

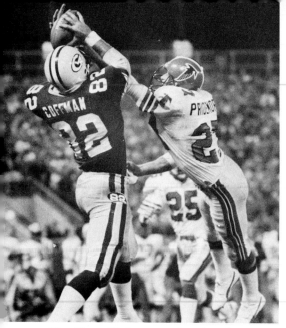

The Starr-Dickey era also saw the development of a big-time, pass-catching tight end, former free agent Paul Coffman.

(Right) Familiar sight: Another touchdown, and Dickey (12) gets congratulations from running back Eddie Lee Ivery.

Joy at last: Fans celebrate the Packers' only postseason victory since 1967, a 41–16 whipping of St. Louis in the first round of the '82 Super Bowl tournament.

Packers' first five draft choices over the next two years, and not only that, he did it without consulting the club's executive committee.

Having made such a bold move without even discussing it with his bosses, Devine had to win big in 1974 — or else. When the Packers went 6–8, Devine saw the handwriting on the wall and took off to accept the head coaching job at Notre Dame.

From that point until 1988, the Packers pursued a course backwards — not only figuratively, but literally. The club reached back into its glorious past for two coaches — Starr and Forrest Gregg — who had been Hall of Fame players for Lombardi.

Neither man could be called a complete bust, but neither could quite get the corner turned, either.

Starr coaxed a 5–3–1 record and a playoff victory from his offensive-minded team in the strike-shortened 1982 season. And he certainly fired up the Lambeau Field scoreboard with points aplenty.

Like Devine before him, Starr traded for an experienced quarterback, but he had far better luck after prying strong-armed Lynn Dickey away from the Houston Oilers. With explosive receivers like James Lofton and John Jefferson running deep as his primary targets and the savvy Starr around to design the offense, Dickey unloaded for 21,369 passing yards from 1976–85 — despite missing the entire '78 season with an injury.

Dickey owns two of the club's top three passing-yardage seasons. He threw for a club-record 4,458 in 1983, topping the 3,529 he recorded in 1980. The '83 team scored a whopping 429 points, which would have been even better news if the defense hadn't leaked 439. Three of the Packers' victories in that thrill-a-minute, 8–8 season came by scores of 41–38, 48–47 and 31–28.

There was certainly plenty of excitement during that abbreviated playoff season in '82. After advancing to what the league dubbed its "Super Bowl tournament," the Packers won their first postseason game since 1967 when they thrashed St. Louis 41–16 at Lambeau Field.

Dickey threw four touchdown passes that day, two of them to Jefferson, and the Packers moved along to a second-round matchup at Dallas. Green Bay lost that one 37–26, but not before rolling up 466 yards of total offense in another wide-open thriller.

Starr's inability to build a defense that might turn all the pyrotechnics into championships, however, ultimately cost him his job. And thus another former hero, Gregg, was brought aboard in 1984.

Gregg already had known some serious coaching success, having pushed Cincinnati into the Super Bowl following the 1981 season. But his first two Green Bay teams went 8–8, after which he made the unfortunate statement that he was tired of playing .500 football and intended to change things. The expected housecleaning didn't have the effect he intended, however, so after 4–12 and 5–9–1 seasons the next two years, Gregg left to take the coaching job at his alma mater, Southern Methodist.

The current Packer president, Harlan, has been with the organization since 1971. Although he didn't ascend to his current position until 1989, he was in a pretty good spot to see what was going wrong through the regimes of Devine, Starr and Gregg.

"This franchise had such incredible success with Lombardi serving in the dual role of coach and general manager that it just seemed that was the way things ought to be done," Harlan said. "One man coached and also ran all the other football business, answering only to the executive committee.

"With all due respect, I think the Packers stuck too long to what had worked in the past, and pro football was changing. We needed somebody else to run the player personnel end of things and let the coach take care of everything on the field."

(Left) The Packers unleashed a pair of dynamic long-ball receivers in the 1980s — John Jefferson (83) and James Lofton (80).

(Above) The Forrest Gregg coaching regime began with high hopes, then floundered with two straight losing seasons. Gregg left for a college coaching job in 1988.

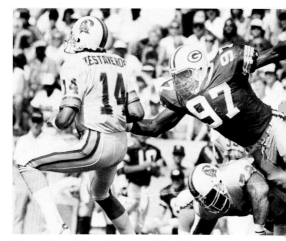

One thing about Forrest Gregg's tenure in Green Bay is that he definitely turned up the pressure on defense, relying on talented, excitable characters like blitzing linebacker Tim Harris (97).

When Lindy Infante took over as coach in 1988, he gave the football to an intriguing young quarterback, Don Majkowski, and the combination clicked just once — with a 10–6 season in 1989.

When the formula finally was changed, it worked only briefly under the first two men chosen to implement it — coach Lindy Infante and Tom Braatz, who was in effect the director of personnel.

Infante, who had been an outstanding offensive coordinator at Cleveland, had a 10–6 season in his second year, 1989, but his other three records were 4–12, 6–10 and 4–12.

All of which set up a massive changing of the guard immediately after a horrible 1991 season in which the Packers lost six of their last eight games. Harlan actually didn't wait for the final game to make his first move, dismissing Braatz in November and hiring Wolf just a week later.

The entire organizational structure was changed, too. Wolf, who long had been considered one of the brightest minds in the NFL, was made executive vice president and general manager, with authority over the entire football operation.

"That was first thing I told Ron when we talked about the job," Harlan said. "I promised him that, in football matters, there would be no interference. He had a blank check."

Wolf tested his authority almost immediately. The '91 season had barely ended when he asked Harlan: "Did you really mean what you said about no interference?"

Assured that would be the case, Wolf promptly fired Infante — which meant buying out the remainder of his contract. It was the type of move which wouldn't have been permitted in the past, but Harlan and the executive committee were determined to let Wolf take the Packers into the mid-1990s with his own type of team.

And quickly enough, along came Holmgren.

Thus the Packers' football brain trust now consists of men who helped build teams with enormous winning traditions — Wolf during a long tenure working for Al Davis and the Raiders, Holmgren as an assistant to Bill Walsh and George Seifert in San Francisco. Those two organizations combined to win seven Super Bowls since Green Bay last played in one.

"The Packers are now in the best hands they could possibly be in," said Nitschke, the old warhorse who has remained a fixture in the Green Bay area. "These are smart guys and they're committed to building a winner. I don't have any doubt they're going to do it and make a lot of noise while they do."

The Packers certainly proved that in the off-season after the surprising 1992 turnaround. They stunned the football world by luring the free agent White, a perennial all-pro with the Eagles who was wooed by several teams — including the 49ers and Redskins. To pull off their coup, the Packers agreed to a four-year, $17 million contract.

If that doesn't represent a commitment to reaching for the brass ring, nothing does.

"I think every team was shocked I picked Green Bay," White said. "(But) this team had always been in the back of my mind. I'm glad to be a Packer."

White took a tour of the Packer Hall of Fame on a trip to Green Bay. Surrounded by artifacts of past triumphs, he admitted he was moved by the team's overwhelming tradition.

And he joked that he'd made a deal with Holmgren: Reggie would sign if the Packers would get him a Super Bowl ring.

"We're going to win," Holmgren has said over and over. "I'm not the sort of person who predicts that we'll be in the Super Bowl this year or that year, but we will win. Everybody here now is focused on that — not just playing to win a few, or win the division, but winning it all.

"That's what we're here for."

After participating in his first summer minicamp with the Packers, White seemed even more enthused — and impressed with how the entire organization was treating his addition to the cast.

"They're making me feel as though I'm not the answer to the problems of the Green Bay Packers," White said. "I believe that if I wouldn't have signed here, the Packers still would have had a chance to win because they were making strides at the end of the year.

"They're making their team better by going out and signing people and through the draft. That's something to feel real confident about."

Favre is convinced.

"Green Bay has waited long enough," he said. "I wouldn't want to be anywhere else. This place is ready to explode. If we get to the Super Bowl, they'd probably shut down the whole state.

"I know it's easy to get carried away too soon. We've still got a lot to learn and lot to prove. We're still getting used to Coach Holmgren's system. We haven't even won a division yet. But I'll be honest: The

The future is now: The current men under the gun are coach Mike Holmgren and quarterback Brett Favre (4).

The present-day Packers are loading up with weapons to complement Favre and receiver Sterling Sharpe. Swift and rugged tight end Jackie Harris caught 55 passes in 1992.

potential is here, the talent and the kind of players who can take this team to the next level.

"And we'll be here awhile. Look around at how young we are. I'm only 23. There are plenty of other young guys, too, and now we have some great veterans like Reggie White and those people to give us just the right kind of balance.

"It's silly to make promises, but I will say our expectations for the future are high. Very high."

Wolf, for one, believes there's a matter of destiny involved — that the Green Bay Packers fully deserve another run with football's elite. He burns to uphold that tradition.

During the 1992 season, the Packers brought several of their great players from other eras back to town, to meet the current players and put them in touch with the brilliant legacy they'd inherited. Even Hornung, the Golden Boy himself, returned to address these young Packers before a game.

Why not let Wolf summarize this proud franchise's view of the future?

"The first thing we show our new players is the old stadium at East High School," he said. "Think of all the success through 75 years. We want these new guys to realize that a lot of great players made history in Green Bay, and we owe them a debt.

"We can only repay that debt by being great again." ❖

Statistics
and
Records

*Players listed below are those who have been active
for at least one league game with the Packers.*

A

Aberson, Cliff (B), No College 1946
Abrams, Nate (E), No College 1921
Abramson, George (T), Minnesota 1925
Acks, Ron (LB), Arizona State 1974–76
Adams, Chet (T), Ohio State 1942–43
Adderley, Herb (B), Michigan State 1961–69
Adkins, Bob (B), Marshall 1940–41, 45–46
Affholter, Erik (WR), Southern Calif. ••1989–91
Afflis, Dick (G), Nevada 1951–54
Agajanian, Ben (K), New Mexico 1961
Albrecht, Art (T), Wisconsin 1941
Aldridge, Ben (B), Oklahoma A&M 1953
Aldridge, Lionel (DE), Utah State 1963–71
Allerman, Kurt (LB), Penn State 1980–81
Amundsen, Norm (G), Wisconsin 1957
Amsler, Marty (DE), Evansville 1970
Anderson, Aric (LB), Millikin 1987
Anderson, Bill (E), Tennessee 1965–66
Anderson, Donny (B), Texas Tech 1966–71
Anderson, John (LB), Michigan 1978–89
Anderson, Vickey Ray (FB), Oklahoma 1980
Ane, Charlie (C), Michigan State 1981
Apsit, Marger (B), Southern Calif. 1932
Archambeau, Lester (DE), Stanford 1990–92
Ard, Billy (G/T), Wake Forest 1989–91
Ariey, Mike (T), San Diego State 1989
Ashmore, Roger (T), Gonzaga 1928–29
Askson, Bert (TE), Texas Southern 1975–77
Atkins, Steve (B), Maryland 1979–81
Auer, Todd (LB), Western Illinois 1987
Austin, Hise (DB), Prairie View A&M 1973
Avery, Steve (FB), Northern Michigan 1991
Aydelette, Buddy (T), Alabama 1980–81

B

Bailey, Byron (B), Washington State 1953
Bain, Bill (T), Southern Calif. 1975
Baker, Frank (E), Northwestern 1931
Baker, Roy (B), Southern Calif. 1928–29
Balazs, Frank (B), Iowa 1939–41
Baldwin, Al (E), Arkansas 1950
Banet, Herb (B), Manchester 1937
Barber, Bob (DE), Grambling 1976–79
Barnes, Emery (E), Oregon 1956
Barnes, Gary (E), Clemson 1962–63
Barnett, Solon (T), Baylor 1945–46
Barragar, Nate (C), Southern Calif. 1931–35
Barrett, Jan (E), Fresno State 1963
Barrie, Sebastian (DE), Liberty Univ. 1992
Barry, Al (G), Southern Calif. 1954–57
Barry, Norm (B), Notre Dame 1921
Barton, Don (B), Texas 1953
Barzilauskas, Carl (DT), Indiana 1978–79
Basing, Myrt (B), Lawrence 1923–27
Basinger, Mike (DE), Cal-Riverside 1974
Baxter, Lloyd (T), Southern Methodist 1948
Beach, Sanjay (WR), Colorado State 1992
Beasley, John (B), South Dakota 1924
Beck, Ken (T), Texas A&M 1959–60
Becker, Wayland (E), Marquette 1936–38
Beekley, Bruce (LB), Oregon 1980

Bell, Albert (WR), Alabama 1988
Bell, Ed (G), Indiana 1947–49
Bennett, Earl (G), Hardin-Simmons 1946
Bennett, Edgar (RB), Florida State 1992
Bennett, Tony (LB), Mississippi 1990–92
Berezney, Paul (T), Fordham 1942–44
Berrang, Ed (E), Villanova 1952
Berry, Connie (E), North Carolina State . . . 1940
Bettencourt, Larry (C), St. Mary's 1933
Bettis, Tom (LB), Purdue 1955–61
Beverly, David (P), Auburn 1975–80
Bilda, Dick (B), Marquette 1944
Billups, Lewis (CB), North Alabama 1992
Biolo, John (G), Lake Forest 1939
Birney, Tom (K), Michigan State 1979–80
Blaine, Ed (G), Missouri 1962
Bland, Carl (WR), Virginia Union 1989–90
Bloodgood, El (B), Nebraska 1930
Boedeker, Bill (B), Kalamazoo 1950
Boerio, Chuck (LB), Illinois 1952
Bolton, Scott (WR), Auburn 1988
Bone, Warren (LB), Texas Southern 1987
Bookout, Billy (B), Austin 1955–56
Boone, J.R. (B), Tulsa 1953
Borak, Fritz (E), Creighton 1938
Borden, Nate (E), Indiana 1955–59
Bowdoin, Jim (G), Alabama 1928–32
Bowman, Ken (C), Wisconsin 1964–73
Boyarsky, Jerry (NT), Pittsburgh 1986–89
Boyd, Elmo (WR), Eastern Kentucky 1978
Boyd, Greg (DE), San Diego State 1983
Bracken, Don (P), Michigan 1985–90
Brackins, Charlie (B), Prairie View A&M . . 1955
Bradley, Dave (G), Penn State 1969–71
Brady, Jeff (LB), Kentucky 1992
Braggs, Byron (DT), Alabama 1981–83
Branstetter, Kent (G/T), Houston 1973
Bratkowski, Zeke (QB), Georgia 1963–68, 71
Bray, Ray (G), Western Michigan 1952

Breen, Gene (LB), Virginia Tech 1964
Brennan, John (G), Michigan 1939
Brock, Charley (C), Nebraska 1939–47
Brock, Lou (B), Purdue 1940–45
Brock, Matt (DE), Oregon 1989–92
Brockington, John (RB), Ohio State 1971–77
Brooks, Robert (WR), South Carolina 1992
Broussard, Steve (P), Southern Miss. 1975
Brown, Aaron (DE), Minnesota 1973–74
Brown, Allen (E), Mississippi 1966–67
Brown, Bill (G), Arkansas 1953–56
Brown, Bob (DT), Arkansas AM&N 1966–73
Brown, Carlos (QB), Pacific 1975–76
Brown, Dave (CB), Michigan . . . . . . ••• 1987–90
Brown, Ken (C), New Mexico 1980
Brown, Robert (LB/DE), Virginia Tech . 1982–92
Brown, Tim (B), Ball State 1959
Brown, Tom (HB), Maryland 1964–68
Browner, Ross (NT), Notre Dame 1987
Bruder, Hank (B), Northwestern 1931–39
Bucchianeri, Mike (G), Indiana 1941, 44–45
Buchanon, Willie (DB), San Diego State 1972–78
Buck, Cub (T), Wisconsin 1921–25
Buckley, Terrell (CB), Florida State 1992
Buhler, Larry (B), Minnesota 1939–41
Buland, Walt (T), No College 1924
Bullough, Hank (G), Michigan State . . . 1955, 58
Bultman, Art (C), Marquette 1932–34
Burgess, Ronnie (DB), Wake Forest 1985
Burnette, Reggie (LB), Houston 1991
Burris, Paul (G), Oklahoma 1949–51
Burrow, Curtis (K), Central Arkansas 1988
Burrow, Jim (DB), Nebraska 1976
Bush, Blair (C), Washington 1989–91
Butler, Bill (B), Chattanooga 1959
Butler, Frank (C), Michigan State . . . 1934–36, 38
Butler, LeRoy (CB/S), Florida State 1990–92
Butler, Mike (DE), Kansas 1977–82, 85

C

Cabral, Brian (LB), Colorado 1980
Cade, Mossy (DB), Texas 1985–86
Caffey, Lee Roy (LB), Texas A&M 1964–69
Cahoon, Ivan (T), Gonzaga 1926–29
Caldwell, David (NT), Texas Christian 1987
Campbell, Rich (QB), California 1981–84
Campen, James (C), Tulane 1989–92
Canadeo, Tony (B), Gonzaga . . 1941, 44, 46–52
Cannava, Al (B), Boston College 1950
Cannon, Mark (C), Texas-Arlington 1985–89
Capp, Dick (LB), Boston College 1967
Capuzzi, Jim (B), Cincinnati 1955–56
Carey, Joe (G), No College 1921
Carlson, Dean (QB), Iowa State 1974
Carlson, Irv (G), St. John's 1926
Carmichael, Al (B), Southern Calif. 1953–58
Carpenter, Lew (B), Arkansas 1959–63
Carr, Fred (LB), Texas-El Paso 1968–77
Carreker, Alphonso (DE), Florida State . 1984–88
Carroll, Leo (DE), San Diego State 1968
Carruth, Paul Ott (RB), Alabama 1986–88
Carter, Carl (CB), Texas Tech 1992
Carter, Jim (LB), Minnesota 1970–78
Carter, Joe (E), Southern Methodist 1942
Carter, Mike (WR), Sacramento State . . . 1970–71

Casper, Charley (B), Texas Christian 1934
Cassidy, Ron (WR), Utah State ****1979–84
Cecil, Chuck (S), Arizona 1988–92
Chandler, Don (K), Florida 1965–67
Cheek, Louis (T), Texas A&M 1991
Cherry, Bill (C), Middle Tenn. State 1986–87
Chesley, Francis (LB), Wyoming 1978
Cheyunski, Jim (LB), Syracuse 1977
Childs, Henry (TE), Kansas State 1984
Choate, Putt (LB), Southern Methodist ... 1987
Christman, Paul (B), Missouri 1950
Cifelli, Gus (T), Notre Dame 1953
Cifers, Bob (B), Tennessee 1949
Clancy, Jack (WR), Michigan 1970
Clanton, Chuck (DB), Auburn 1985
Claridge, Dennis (QB), Nebraska 1964–65
Clark, Allan (RB), Northern Arizona 1982
Clark, Greg (LB), Arizona State 1991
Clark, Jessie (FB), Arkansas 1983–87
Clark, Vinnie (CB), Ohio State 1991–92
Clemens, Bob (B), Georgia 1955
Clemens, Cal (B), Southern Calif. 1936
Clemons, Ray (G), St. Mary's 1947
Cloud, Jack (B), William & Mary 1950–51
Cody, Ed (B), Purdue 1947–48
Coffey, Junior (RB), Washington 1965
Coffman, Paul (TE), Kansas State 1978–85
Collier, Steve (T), Bethune Cookman ... 1987–88
Collins, Al (B), Louisiana State 1951
Collins, Brett (LB), Washington 1992
Collins, Patrick (RB), Oklahoma 1988
Comp, Irv (B), St. Benedict 1943–49
Compton, Chuck (DB), Boise State 1987
Comstock, Rudy (G), Georgetown 1931–33
Concannon, Jack (QB), Boston College 1974
Conway, Dave (G), Texas 1971
Cone, Fred (B), Clemson 1951–57
Cook, Jim (G), Wisconsin 1921
Cook, Kelly (RB), Oklahoma State 1987
Cook, Ted (E), Alabama 1948–50
Cooke, Bill (DE), Massachusetts 1975
Cooney, Mark (DE), Colorado 1974
Corker, John (LB), Oklahoma State 1988
Coughlin, Frank (B), Notre Dame 1921
Coutre, Larry (B), Notre Dame 1950, 53
Craig, Larry (B), South Carolina 1939–49
Cremer, Ted (E), Auburn 1948
Crenshaw, Leon (DT), Tuskegee 1968
Crimmins, Bernie (G), Notre Dame 1945
Croft, Milburn (T), Ripon 1942–47
Cronin, Tom (B), Marquette 1922
Croston, Dave (T), Iowa .... +++1987–89
Crouse, Ray (RB), Nevada-Las Vegas 1984
Crowley, Jim (B), Notre Dame 1925
Crutcher, Tommy (LB), TCU 1964–67, 71–72
Cuff, Ward (B), Marquette 1947
Culbreath, Jim (FB), Oklahoma 1977–79
Culver, Al (T), Notre Dame 1932
Curcio, Mike (LB), Temple 1983
Currie, Dan (LB), Michigan State 1958–64
Curry, Bill (C), Georgia Tech 1965–66
Cumby, George (LB), Oklahoma 1980–85
Cvercko, Andy (G), Northwestern 1960
Cyre, Hector (T), Gonzaga 1926–28

D

Dahms, Tom (T), San Diego State 1955
Dale, Carroll (WR), Virginia Tech 1965–72
Danelo, Joe (K), Washington State 1975
Daniell, Averell (T), Pittsburgh 1937

Danjean, Ernie (G), Auburn 1957
Darling, Bernard (C), Beloit 1927–31
Davenport, Bill (B), Hardin-Simmons 1931
Davey, Don (DE), Wisconsin 1991–92
Davidson, Ben (T), Washington 1961
Davis, Dave (WR), Tennessee A&I 1971–72
Davis, Harper (B), Mississippi State 1951
Davis, Kenneth (RB), Texas Christian .. 1986–88
Davis, Paul (G), Marquette 1922
Davis, Ralph (G), Wisconsin 1947–48
Davis, Willie (DE), Grambling 1960–69
Dawson, Dale (K), Eastern Kentucky 1988
Dawson, Gib (B), Texas 1953
Dean, Walter (FB), Grambling.......... 1991
Deeks, Don (T), Texas 1948
Dees, Bob (T), Southwest Missouri State ... 1952
Degrate, Tony (DE), Texas 1985
Del Gaizo, Jim (QB), Tampa 1973
Del Greco, Al (K), Auburn 1984–87
DeLisle, Jim (DT), Wisconsin 1971
De Luca, Tony (NT), Rhode Island 1984
DeMoe, Bill (E), Beloit 1921
Dennard, Preston (WR), New Mexico 1985
Dent, Burnell (LB), Tulane 1986–92
Deschaine, Dick (E), No College 1955–57
Detmer, Ty (QB), Brigham Young 1992
Dickey, Lynn (QB), Kansas State *1976–85
Didier, Clint (TE), Portland State 1988–89
Dillon, Bobby (B), Texas 1952–59
Dilweg, Anthony (QB), Duke 1989–90
Dilweg, Lavvie (E), Marquette 1927–34
Dimler, Rich (T), Southern Calif. 1980
DiPierro, Ray (G), Ohio State 1950–51
Disend, Leo (T), Albright 1940
Dittrich, John (G), Wisconsin 1959
Don Carlos, John (C), Drake 1931
D'Onofrio, Mark (LB), Penn State 1992
Donohoe, Mike (TE), San Francisco 1973–74
Dorsey, Dean (K), Toronto 1988
Dorsey, John (LB), Connecticut ...... •1984–89
Douglas, George (C), Marquette 1921
Douglass, Bobby (QB), Kansas 1978
Douglass, Mike (LB), San Diego State .. 1978–85
Dowden, Steve (T), Baylor 1952
Dowler, Boyd (E), Colorado 1959–69
Dowling, Brian (QB), Yale 1977
Drechsler, Dave (G), North Carolina ... 1983–84
Dreyer, Wally (B), Wisconsin 1950–51
Drost, Jeff (DT), Iowa 1987
Drulis, Chuck (G), Temple 1950
Duford, Wilfred (B), Marquette 1924
Duhart, Paul (B), Florida 1944
Dunaway, Dave (E), Duke 1968
Duncan, Ken (P/WR), Tulsa 1971
Dunn, Red (B), Marquette 1927–31
Dunningan, Walt (E), Minnesota 1922

E

Earhart, Ralph (B), Texas Tech 1948–49
Earp, Jug (C), Monmouth............. 1922–32
Eason, Roger (T), Oklahoma 1949
Ecker, Ed (T), John Carroll 1950–51
Edwards, Earl (DT), Wichita State 1979
Ellerson, Gary (FB), Wisconsin 1985–86
Elliott, Burton (B), Marquette 1921
Elliott, Carleton (E), Virginia 1951–54
Elliott, Tony (DB), Central Michigan ... 1987–88
Ellis, Gerry (FB), Missouri 1980–86
Ellis, Ken (DB), Southern 1970–75
Enderle, Dick (G), Minnesota 1976

Engebretsen, Tiny (G), Northwestern .. 1934–41
Engelmann, Wuert (B), South Dakota St. 1930–33
Enright, Rex (B), Notre Dame 1926–27
Epps, Phillip (WR), Texas Christian 1982–88
Erickson, Harry (B), Washington & Jefferson 1923
Estep, Mike (G), Bowling Green 1987
Estes, Roy (B), Georgia 1928
Ethridge, Joe (T), Southern Methodist 1949
Evans, Dick (E), Iowa 1940, 43
Evans, John (B), California 1929
Evans, Lon (G), Texas Christian 1933–37

F

Falkenstein, Tony (B), St. Mary's 1943
Fanucci, Mike (DE), Arizona State 1974
Faverty, Hal (C), Wisconsin 1952
Favre, Brett (QB), Southern Mississippi 1992
Faye, Allen (E), Marquette 1922
Feasel, Greg (T), Abilene Christian 1986
Feathers, Beattie (B), Tennessee 1940
Felker, Art (E), Marquette 1951
Ferguson, Howie (B), No College 1953–58
Ferragamo, Vince (QB), Nebraska 1985–86
Ferry, Lou (T), Villanova 1949
Fields, Angelo (T), Michigan State 1982
Finely, Jim (G), Michigan State 1942
Finnin, Tom (T), Detroit 1957
Fitzgerald, Kevin (TE), Wisconsin-Eau Claire 1987
Fitzgibbons, Paul (B), Creighton 1930–32
Flaherty, Dick (E), Marquette 1926–27
Flanigan, Jim (LB), Pittsburgh 1967–70
Fleming, Marv (E), Utah 1963–69
Flowers, Bob (C), Texas Tech 1942–48
Floyd, Bobby Jack (B), Texas Christian . 1952, 54
Flynn, Tom (S), Pittsburgh............ 1984–86
Folkins, Lee (E), Washington.......... 1961
Fontenot, Herman (RB), Louisiana State 1989–90
Ford, Len (E), Michigan 1958
Forester, Bill (LB), Southern Methodist . 1953–63
Forte, Aldo (G), Montana 1947
Forte, Bob (B), Arkansas 1946–53
Francis, Joe (B), Oregon State 1958–60
Frankowski, Bob (G), Washington 1945
Franta, Herb (T), St. Thomas 1930
Franz, Nolan (WR), Tulane 1986
Freeman, Bob (B), Auburn 1959
Fries, Sherwood (G), Colorado State 1943
Fritsch, Ted (B), Stevens Point Teachers' 1942–50
Frutig, Ed (E), Michigan 1941–45
Fuller, Joe (CB), Northern Iowa 1991
Fullwood, Brent (RB), Auburn 1987–90
Fusina, Chuck (QB), Penn State 1986

G

Gabbard, Steve (T), Florida State 1991
Gantenbein, Milt (E), Wisconsin 1931–40
Garcia, Eddie (K), Southern Methodist . 1983–84
Gardella, Augustus (B), Holy Cross 1922
Gardner, Milt (G), Wisconsin 1922–26

225

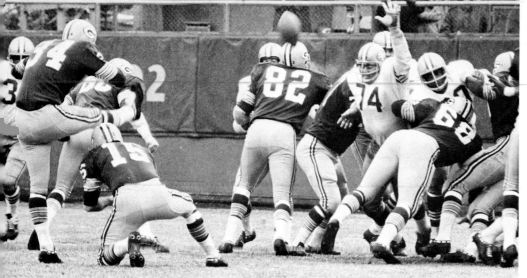

Garrett, Bob (B), Stanford 1954
Garrett, Len (TE), N.M. Highlands 1971–72
Gassert, Ron (T), Virginia 1962
Gatewood, Lester (C), Baylor 1946–47
Gavin, Fritz (E), Marquette 1921, 23
Gaydos, Kent (WR), Florida State 1975
Getty, Charlie (T), Penn State 1983
Gibson, Paul (WR), Texas-El Paso 1972
Gillette, Jim (B), Virginia 1947
Gillingham, Gale (G), Minnesota . . . 1966–74, 76
Gillus, Willie (QB), Norfolk State 1987
Girard, Jug (B), Wisconsin 1948–51
Glass, Leland (WR), Oregon 1972–73
Glick, Eddie (B), Marquette 1921–22
Gofourth, Derrel (C), Oklahoma State . . 1977–82
Goldenberg, Charles (G), Wisconsin . . 1933–45
Goodman, Les (RB), Yankton 1973–74
Goodnight, Clyde (E), Tulsa 1945–49
Gordon, Lou (T), Illinois 1936–37
Gorgal, Ken (B), Purdue 1956
Grabowski, Jim (B), Illinois 1966–70
Gray, Cecil (T), North Carolina 1992
Gray, Jack (E), No College 1923
Gray, Johnnie (DB), Cal St.-Fullerton . . . 1975–84
Green, Jessie (WR), Tulsa 1976
Greene, Tiger (S), Western Carolina 1986–90
Greeney, Norm (G), Notre Dame 1933
Greenfield, Tom (C), Arizona 1939–41
Greenwood, David (DB), Wisconsin . ++1986–87
Gregg, Forrest (T), So. Methodist . . . 1956, 58–70
Gremminger, Hank (B), Baylor 1956–65
Griffen, Harold (C), Iowa 1928
Grimes, Billy (B), Oklahoma A&M 1950–52
Grimm, Dan (G), Colorado 1963–65
Gros, Earl (B), Louisiana State 1962–63
Grove, Roger (B), Michigan State 1931–35
Gruber, Bob (T), Pittsburgh 1987
Gudauskas, Pete (G), Murray State 1942, 45
Gueno, Jim (LB), Tulane 1976–80
Gudie, Walter (G), Wisconsin 1943–44

H

Hackbart, Dale (B), Wisconsin 1960
Hackett, Joey (TE), Elon 1987–88
Haddix, Michael (FB), Mississippi State 1989–90
Hadl, John (QB), Kansas 1974–75
Haley, Darryl (T), Utah 1988
Hall, Charles (DB), Pittsburgh 1971–76
Hall, Mark (DE), Southwestern La. 1989–90
Hallstrom, Ron (G), Iowa 1982–92
Hampton, Dave (RB), Wyoming 1969–71

Hanner, Dave (DT), Arkansas 1952–64
Hanny, Frank (T), Indiana 1930
Hansen, Don (LB), Illinois 1976–77
Hanson, Roy (B), Marquette 1923
Harden, Derrick (WR), East New Mexico . 1987
Harden, Leon (DS), Texas-El Paso 1970
Harding, Roger (C), California 1949
Hardy, Kevin (DT), Notre Dame 1970
Hargrove, James (RB), Wake Forest 1987
Harrell, Willard (RB), Pacific 1975–77
Harris, Corey (WR/KR), Vanderbilt 1992
Harris, Jackie (TE), Northeast La. 1990–92
Harris, John (B), Wisconsin 1925–26
Harris, Leotis (G), Arkansas . . . . ##1978–84
Harris, Tim (LB), Memphis State 1986–90
Harris, William (TE), Bishop College 1990
Harrison, Anthony (DB), Georgia Tech 1987
Harrison, Reggie (RB), Cincinnati 1978
Hart, Doug (DB), Texas-Arlington 1964–71
Hartnett, Perry (G), Southern Methodist . . . 1987
Hartwig, Keith (WR), Arizona 1977
Harvey, Maurice (S), Ball State 1981–83
Hathcock, Dave (B), Memphis State 1966
Hauck, Tim (S), Montana 1991–92
Havig, Dennis (G), Colorado 1977
Haycraft, Ken (E), Wisconsin 1964–66
Hayes, Gary (DB), Fresno State 1984–86
Hayes, Norb (E), Marquette 1923
Hayhoe, Bill (T), Southern Calif. 1969–74
Hays, Dave (E), Notre Dame 1921–22
Hays, George (E), St. Bonaventure 1953
Hearden, Les (B), St. Ambrose 1924
Hearden, Tom (B), Notre Dame 1927–28
Heath, Stan (B), Nevada 1949
Hefner, Larry (LB), Clemson 1972–75
Held, Paul (QB), San Diego State 1955
Helluin, Jerry (T), Tulane 1954–57
Hendrian, Warren (B), Pittsburgh 1924
Hendricks, Ted (LB), Miami (Fla.) 1974
Henry, Urban (T), Georgia Tech 1963
Herber, Arnie (B), Regis 1930–41
Hickman, Larry (B), Baylor 1960
Highsmith, Don (RB), Michigan State 1973
Hill, Don (B), Stanford 1929
Hill, Jim (DB), Texas A&I 1972–74
Hill, Nate (DE), Auburn 1988
Hilton, John (TE), Richmond 1970
Himes, Dick (T), Ohio State 1968–77
Hinkle, Clarke (B), Bucknell 1932–41
Hinte, Tex (E), Pittsburgh 1941
Hobbins, Jim (G), Minnesota 1987

Hoffman, Gary (T), Santa Clara 1984
Holland, Johnny (LB), Texas A&M 1987–92
Holler, Ed (LB), South Carolina 1963
Holmes, Jerry (CB), West Virginia 1990–91
Hood, Estus (DB), Illinois State 1978–84
Horn, Don (QB), San Diego State 1967–70
Hornung, Paul (B), Notre Dame . 1957–62, 64–66
Houston, Bobby (LB), North Carolina St. . . 1990
Howard, Lynn (B), Indiana 1921–22
Howell, John (B), Nebraska 1938
Howton, Bill (E), Rice 1952–58
Hubbard, Cal (T), Centenary, Geneva . 1929–35
Huckleby, Harlan (RB), Michigan 1980–85
Hudson, Bob (RB), Northeastern (Okla.) St. 1972
Hudson, Craig (TE), Wisconsin 1990
Huffman, Tim (T), Notre Dame 1981–85
Hull, Tom (LB), Penn State 1975
Humphrey, Donnie (DE), Auburn 1984–86
Hunt, Ervin (DB), Fresno State 1970
Hunt, Kevin (T), Doane (Neb.) 1972
Hunt, Michael (LB), Minnesota 1978–80
Hunt, Sam (LB), Stephen F. Austin 1980
Hunter, Art (C), Notre Dame 1954
Hunter, Scott (QB), Alabama 1971–73
Hunter, Tony (RB), Minnesota 1987
Hutson, Don (E), Alabama 1935–45
Hyland, Bob (C), Boston College . . . 1967–69, 76

I

Iman, Ken (C), Southeast Mo. State 1960–63
Ingalls, Bob (C), Michigan 1942
Ingram, Darryl (TE), California 1992
Isbell, Cecil (B), Purdue 1938–42
Ivery, Eddie Lee (RB), Georgia Tech . ++1979–87

J

Jacke, Chris (K), Texas-El Paso 1989–92
Jackson, Johnnie (S), Houston 1992
Jackson, Mel (G), Southern Calif. 1976–80
Jacobs, Allen (B), Utah 1965
Jacobs, Jack (B), Oklahoma 1947–49
Jacunski, Harry (E), Fordham 1939–44
Jakes, Van (CB), Kent State 1989
James, Claudis (FL), Jackson State 1967–69
Jankowski, Eddie (B), Wisconsin 1937–41
Jansante, Val (E), Duquesne 1951
Jay, Craig (TE), Mount Senario 1987
Jean, Walter (G), Missouri 1925–26
Jefferson, John (WR), Arizona State 1981–84
Jefferson, Norman (DB), Louisiana State 1987–88
Jenison, Ray (T), South Dakota State 1931
Jenke, Noel (LB), Minnesota 1973–74
Jennings, Jim (E), Missouri 1955
Jensen, Greg (G), No College 1987
Jensen, Jim (RB), Iowa 1981–82
Jeter, Bob (DB), Iowa 1963–70
Johnson, Bill (E), Minnesota 1941
Johnson, Charles (DT), Maryland . . . 1979–80, 83
Johnson, Danny (LB), Tennessee State 1978
Johnson, Ezra (DE), Morris Brown 1977–87
Johnson, Glen (T), Arizona State 1949
Johnson, Howard (G), Georgia 1940–41
Johnson, Joe (B), Boston College 1954–58
Johnson, Kenneth (DB), Miss. State ++++1987–88
Johnson, Marv (B), San Jose State 1952–53
Johnson, Randy (QB), Texas A&I 1976
Johnson, Sammy Lee (B), North Carolina . . 1979
Johnson, Tom (T), Michigan 1952
Johnston, Chester (B), Marquette 1934–39
Johnstone, Art (B), Lawrence 1931

Jolly, Mike (S), Michigan 1980–83
Jones, Bob (G), Indiana 1934
Jones, Bruce (G), Alabama 1927–28
Jones, Daryll (DB), Georgia 1984–85
Jones, Ron (TE), Texas-El Paso 1969
Jones, Scott (T), Washington 1991
Jones, Terry (DL), Alabama 1978–84
Jones, Tom (G), Bucknell 1938
Jordan, Henry (DT), Virginia 1959–69
Jordan, Kenneth (LB), Tuskegee 1987
Jorgenson, Carl (T), St. Mary's 1934
Jurkovic, John (NT), Eastern Illinois . . . 1991–92

K

Kahler, Bob (B), Nebraska 1941–44
Kahler, Royal (T), Nebraska 1942
Kalosh, Mike (E), La Crosse St. Teachers . . . 1948
Katalinas, Leo (T), Catholic Univ. 1938
Kauahi, Kani (C), Hawaii 1988
Keane, Jim (E), Iowa 1952
Keefe, Emmett (T), Notre Dame 1921
Kekeris, Jim (T), Missouri 1948
Kell, Paul (T), Notre Dame 1939–40
Kelley, Bill (E), Texas Tech 1949
Kemp, Perry (WR), California (Pa.) Univ 1988–91
Kenyon, Crowell (G), Ripon 1923
Kercher, Bob (E), Georgetown 1944
Kern, Bill (T), Pittsburgh 1929–30
Keuper, Ken (B), Georgia 1945–47
Kiel, Blair (QB), Notre Dame 1988–91
Kiesling, Walt (T), St. Thomas 1935–36
Kilbourn, Warren (T), Michigan 1939
Kimball, Bob (WR), Oklahoma 1979–80
Kimmel, J.D. (T), Houston 1958
Kinard, Bill (B), Mississippi 1957–58
King, David (DB), Auburn 1987
King, Don (T), Kentucky 1956
King, Don (DB), Southern Methodist 1987
Kirby, John (B), Southern Calif. 1949
Kitson, Syd (G), Wake Forest ****1980–84
Klaus, Fee (C), No College 1921
Kliebhan, Adolph (B), Milwaukee Teachers 1921
Koart, Matt (LB), Southern Calif. 1986
Koch, Greg (T), Arkansas 1977–85
Koncar, Mark (T), Colorado ****1976–82
Koonce, George (LB), East Carolina 1992
Kopay, Dave (B), Washington 1972
Knafelc, Gary (E), Colorado 1954–62
Knutson, Gene (E), Michigan 1954–56
Knutson, Steve (T), Southern Calif. 1976–77
Konopasek, Ed (T), Ball State 1987
Kostelnik, Ron (T), Cincinnati 1961–68
Kotal, Eddie (B), Lawrence 1925–29
Kovatch, John (E), Notre Dame 1947
Kowalkowski, Bob (G), Virginia 1977
Kramer, Jerry (G), Idaho 1958–68
Kramer, Ron (TE), Michigan 1957, 59–64
Kranz, Ken (B), Milwaukee Teachers 1949
Krause, Larry (RB), St. Norbert 1970–74
Kresky, Joe (G), Wisconsin 1930
Kroll, Bob (DB), Northern Michigan . . . 1972–73
Kuechenberg, Rudy (LB), Indiana 1970
Kuick, Stan (G), Beloit 1926
Kurth, Joe (T), Notre Dame 1933–34
Kuusisto, Bill (G), Minnesota 1941–46

L

Laabs, Kermit (B), Beloit 1929
Labbe, Rico (S), Boston College 1990
Ladrow, Wally (B), No College 1921

Lally, Bob (LB), Cornell 1976
Lambeau, Earl "Curly" (B), Notre Dame 1921–30
Lammons, Pete (TE), Texas 1972
Lande, Cliff (E), Carroll 1921
Landers, Walt (RB), Clark College 1978–79
Lane, MacArthur (RB), Utah State 1972–74
Lankas, Jim (B), St. Mary's 1943
Larson, Bill (TE), Colorado State 1980
Larson, Fred (C), Notre Dame 1925
Larson, Kurt (LB), Michigan State 1991
Laslavic, Jim (LB), Penn State 1982
Lathrop, Kit (DT), Arizona State 1979–80
Lauer, John (B), Detroit 1922
Lauer, Larry (C), Alabama 1956–57
Laughlin, Jim (LB), Ohio State 1983
Lawrence, Jim (B), Texas Christian 1939
Laws, Joe (B), Iowa 1934–45
Leaper, Wesley (E), Wisconsin 1921, 23
Lee, Bill (T), Alabama 1937–42, 46
Lee, Mark (CB), Washington 1980–90
Leigh, Charlie (RB), No College 1974
Leiker, Tony (DE), Stanford 1987
Leopold, Bobby (LB), Notre Dame . . . ++1986–87
Lester, Darrell (C), Texas Christian 1937–38
Letlow, Russ (G), San Francisco 1936–42, 46
Lewellen, Verne (B), Nebraska 1924–32
Lewis, Cliff (LB), Southern Miss. 1981–84
Lewis, Gary (TE), Texas–Arlington 1981–84
Lewis, Mark (TE), Texas A&M 1985–87
Lewis, Mike (NT), Arkansas A&M 1980
Lewis, Ron (WR), Florida State 1992
Lewis, Tim (CB), Pittsburgh 1983–86
Lidberg, Carl (B), Minnesota 1926–30
Lipscomb, Paul (T), Tennessee 1945–49
Liscio, Tony (T), Tulsa 1963
Livingston, Dale (K), Western Michigan . . . 1970
Lofton, James (WR), Stanford 1978–86
Logan, David (NT), Pittsburgh 1987
Logan, Dick (T), Ohio State 1952–53
Lollar, George (B), Howard 1928

Long, Bob (E), Wichita 1964–67
Loomis, Ace (B), La Crosse St. Teachers 1951–53
Losch, John (B), Miami (Fla.) 1956
Lucky, Bill (T), Baylor 1955
Ludtke, Norm (G), Carroll 1924
Lueck, Bill (G), Arizona 1968–74
Luhn, Nolan (E), Tulsa 1945–49
Luke, Steve (DB), Ohio State 1975–80
Lusteg, Booth (K), Connecticut 1969–70
Lyle, Dewey (E), Minnesota 1922–23
Lyman, Del (T), UCLA 1941

M

MacAuliffe, John (B), Beloit 1926
Mack, "Red" (E), Notre Dame 1966
MacLeod, Tom (LB), Minnesota 1973
Maddox, George (T), Kansas State 1935
Majkowski, Don (QB), Virginia 1987–92
Malancon, Rydell (LB), Louisiana State 1987
Malone, Grover (B), Notre Dame 1921
Mandarich, Tony (T), Michigan St. ••••1989–92
Mandeville, Chris (DB), California-Davis1987–88
Manley, Leon (G), Oklahoma 1950–51
Mann, Bob (E), Michigan 1950–54
Mann, Erroll (K), North Dakota 1968, 76
Mansfield, Von (DB), Wisconsin 1987
Marcol, Chester (K), Hillsdale 1972–80
Marks, Larry (B), Indiana 1928
Marshall, Rich (T), Stephen F. Austin 1965
Martell, Herman (E), No College 1921
Martin, Charles (DE), Livingston 1984–87
Martinkovic, John (E), Xavier 1951–56
Mason, Dave (DB), Nebraska 1974
Mason, Joel (E), Western Michigan 1941–45
Mason, Larry (RB), Troy State 1988
Massey, Carlton (E), Texas 1957–58
Masters, Norm (T), Michigan State 1957–64
Mataele, Stan (LB), Arizona 1987
Mathys, Charley (B), Indiana 1922–26
Matson, Pat (G), Oregon 1975

227

Matthews, Al (DB), Texas A&I 1970–75
Matthews, Aubrey (WR), Delta State . . . 1988–89
Mattos, Harry (B), St. Mary's 1936
Matuszak, Marv (LB), Tulsa 1958
Mayer, Frank (G), Notre Dame 1927
McBride, Ron (RB), Missouri 1973
McCaffrey, Bob (C), Southern Calif. 1975
McCarren, Larry (C), Illinois 1973–84
McCloughan, Dave (CB), Colorado 1992
McConkey, Phil (WR), Navy 1986
McCoy, Mike C. (DB), Colorado . . . . ##1976–84
McCoy, Mike P. (DT), Notre Dame 1970–76
McCrary, Hurdis (B), Georgia 1929–33
McDougal, Bob (B), Miami (Fla.) 1947
McDowell, John (G), St. John's 1964
McGarry, John (G), St. Joseph's 1987
McGaw, Walter (G), Beloit 1926
McGeary, Clink (T), North Dakota 1950
McGee, Buford (FB), Mississippi 1992
McGee, Max (E), Tulane 1954, 57–67
McGeorge, Rich (TE), Elon 1970–78
McGrew, Sylvester (DE), Tulane 1987
McGruder, Michael (CB), Kent State 1989
McHan, Lamar (B), Arkansas 1959–60
McIlhenny, Don (B), So. Methodist 1957–59
McJulien, Paul (P), Jackson State 1991–92
McKay, Roy (B), Texas 1944–47
McLaughlin, Joe (LB), Massachusetts 1979
McLaughlin, Lee (G), Virginia 1941
McLean, Ray (B), No College 1921
McLeod, Mike (DB), Montana State 1984–85
McMath, Herb (OL), Morningside 1977
McMillan, Ernie (T), Illinois 1975
McNabb, Dexter (FB), Florida 1992
McNally (Blood), Johnny (B), St. John's . 1928–36
McPartland, Bill (T), Texas 1947
McPherson, Forrest (T), Nebraska 1943–45
Meade, Mike (FB), Penn State 1982–83
Meilinger, Steve (E), Kentucky 1958–60
Melka, James (LB), Wisconsin 1987
Mendenhall, Ken (C), Oklahoma 1970
Mendoza, Ruben (G), Wayne State 1986–89
Mercein, Chuck (B), Yale 1967–69
Mercer, Mike (K), Northern Arizona . . . 1968–69
Merrill, Casey (DE), California-Davis . . 1979–83
Merrill, Mark (LB), Minnesota 1982
Mestnik, Frank (B), Marquette 1963
Meyer, Jim (T), Illinois State 1987
Michaels, Lou (K), Kentucky 1971
Michaels, Walt (G), Washington & Lee . . . 1951
Michalske, Mike (G), Penn State 1929–37
Middleton, Terdell (RB), Memphis State 1977–81
Midler, Lou (G), Minnesota 1941
Mihajlovich, Lou (B), Indiana 1954
Miketinac, Nick (G), St. Norbert 1937
Milan, Don (QB), Cal Poly-San Luis Obispo 1975
Millard, Keith (DE), Washington State . . . 1992
Miller, Charles (C), Purdue 1938
Miller, Don (B), Wisconsin 1941–42
Miller, Don (B), Southern Methodist 1954
Miller, John (T), Boston College 1960
Miller, John (LB), Mississippi State 1987
Miller, Mark (QB), Bowling Green 1980
Miller, Paul (B), South Dakota 1936–38
Miller, Tom (E), Hampden-Sydney 1946
Mills, Tom (B), Penn State 1922–23
Milton, Tom (E), Lake Forest 1924
Minick, Paul (G), Iowa 1928–29
Mitchell, Charles (B), Tulsa 1946
Mitchell, Roland (CB/S), Texas Tech . . . 1991–92

Moffitt, Mike (WR), Fresno State 1986
Moje, Dick (E), Loyola (Calif.) 1951
Molenda, Bo (B), Michigan 1929–32
Monaco, Ron (LB), South Carolina 1987
Monnett, Bobby (B), Michigan State 1933–38
Monroe, Henry (DB), Mississippi State . . . 1979
Moore, Allen (E), Texas A&M 1939
Moore, Blake (C/G), Wooster 1984–85
Moore, Brent (DE), Southern Calif. ####1987–88
Moore, Rich (DT), Villanova 1969–70
Moore, Tom (B), Vanderbilt 1960–65
Moran, Rich (G), San Diego State 1985–92
Moresco, Tim (DB), Syracuse 1977
Morris, Jim Bob (DB), Kansas State 1987
Morris, Larry (RB), Syracuse 1987
Morris, Lee (WR), Oklahoma 1987
Moselle, Dom (B), Superior State 1951–52
Mosley, Russ (B), Alabama 1945–46
Moss, Perry (B), Illinois 1948
Mott, Norm (B), Georgia 1933
Mulleneaux, Carl (E), Utah State 1938–41, 45–46
Mulleneaux, Lee (T), Northern Arizona . . . 1938
Murphy, Mark (S), West Liberty St. ###1980–91
Murray, Dick (T), Marquette 1921–24

N

Nadolney, Romanus (G), Notre Dame 1922
Nash, Tom (E), Georgia 1928–32
Neal, Ed (G/C), Tulane 1945–51
Neal, Frankie (WR), Fort Hays State 1987
Neill, Bill (NT), Pittsburgh 1984
Nelson, Bob (NT), Miami (Fla.) 1988–90
Neville, Tom (T/G), Fresno State . . . 1986–88, 92
Nichols, Ham (G), Rice 1951
Niemann, Walt (C), Michigan 1922–24
Nitschke, Ray (LB), Illinois 1958–72
Nix, Doyle (B), Southern Methodist 1955
Nixon, Fred (WR), Oklahoma ****1980–82
Noble, Brian (LB), Arizona State 1985–92
Noonan, Danny (NT), Nebraska 1992
Norgard, Al (E), Stanford 1934
Norseth, Mike (QB), Kansas 1990
Norton, Jerry (DB), So. Methodist 1963–64
Norton, Martin (B), Carleton 1925–28
Nussbaumer, Bob (B), Michigan 1946
Nuzum, Rick (C), Kentucky **1978–79
Nystrom, Lee (T), Macalester 1973–74

O

Oakes, Bill (T), Haskell 1921
Oates, Brad (T), Brigham Young 1981
Oats, Carleton (DT), Florida A&M 1973
O'Boyle, Harry (B), Notre Dame 1928–29, 32
O'Connor, Bob (T), Stanford 1935
Odom, Steve (WR), Utah 1974–79
O'Donahue, Pat (E), Wisconsin 1955
O'Donnell, Dick (E), Minnesota 1924–30
Odson, Urban (T), Minnesota 1946–49
Oglesby, Alfred (NT), Houston 1992
Ohlgren, Earl (E), Minnesota 1942
Okoniewski, Steve (DT), Montana 1974–75
Olsen, Ralph (E), Utah 1949
Olsonoski, Larry (G), Minnesota 1948–49
O'Malley, Jack (T), Southern Calif. 1970
O'Malley, Tom (QB), Cincinnati 1950
O'Neil, Ed (LB), Penn State 1980
Orlich, Dan (E), Nevada 1949–51
Osborn, Dave (RB), North Dakota 1976
O'Steen, Dwayne (CB), San Jose State . . . 1983–84
Owens, Henry (G), Lake Forest 1922

P

Palumbo, Sam (G), Notre Dame 1957
Pannell, Ernie (T), Texas A&M 1941–42, 45
Pape, Orrin (B), Iowa 1930
Papit, John (B), Virginia 1953
Parilli, Babe (QB), Kentucky 1952–53, 56–58
Parker, Freddie (RB), Miss. Valley St. 1987
Paskett, Keith (WR), Western Kentucky . . . 1987
Paskvan, George (B), Wisconsin 1941
Pass, Randy (LB), Georgia Tech 1978
Patrick, Frank (QB), Nebraska 1970–72
Patterson, Shawn (DE), Arizona State &1988–92
Patton, Ricky (B), Jackson State 1979
Paulekas, Tony (C), Washington & Jefferson 1936
Paup, Bryce (LB), Northern Iowa 1990–92
Payne, Ken (WR), Langston 1974–77
Pearson, Lindell (B), Oklahoma 1952
Peay, Francis (T), Missouri 1968–72
Pelfrey, Ray (E), East Kentucky State . . . 1951–52
Perkins, Don (B), Platteville St. Teachers 1943–45
Perko, Tom (LB), Pittsburgh 1976
Perry, Claude (T), Alabama 1927–35
Pesonen, Dick (B), Minnesota-Duluth 1960
Peterson, Les (E), Texas 1932–35
Peterson, Phil (B), Wisconsin 1932
Peterson, Ray (B), San Francisco 1937
Petitbon, John (B), Notre Dame 1957
Petway, David (S), Northern Illinois 1981
Pisarkiewicz, Steve (QB), Missouri 1980
Pitts, Elijah (B), Philander Smith . . . 1961–69, 71
Pitts, Ron (CB), UCLA 1988–90
Ploeger, Kurt (DE), Gustavus Adolphus . . . 1986
Pointer, John (LB), Vanderbilt 1987
Pope, Bucky (E), Catawba 1968
Powers, Sam (G), Northern Michigan 1921
Prather, Guy (LB), Grambling 1981–85
Pregulman, Merv (G), Michigan 1946
Prescott, Ace (E), Hardin-Simmons 1946
Priatko, Bill (G), Pittsburgh 1957
Pritko, Steve (E), Villanova 1949–50
Prokop, Joe (P), Cal Poly-San Luis Obispo . 1985
Provo, Fred (B), Washington 1948
Psaltis, Jim (B), Southern Calif. 1954
Purdy, Pid (B), Beloit 1926–27
Pureifory, Dave (DL), Eastern Michigan 1972–77
Purnell, Frank (B), Alcorn A&M 1957
Putman, Earl (C), Arizona State 1957

Q

Quatse, Jess (T), Pittsburgh 1933
Query, Jeff (WR), Millikin 1989–91
Quinlan, Bill (E), Michigan State 1959–62

R

Radick, Ken (E), Marquette 1930–31
Rafferty, Vince (C), Colorado 1987
Randolph, Al (DB), Iowa 1971
Randolph, Terry (DB), American Intern'l . . 1977
Ranspot, Keith (E), Southern Methodist . . . 1942
Rash, Louis (DB), Mississippi Valley St. . . . 1987
Ray, Baby (T), Vanderbilt 1938–48
Redick, Cornelius (WR), Cal St.-Fullerton . . 1987
Regnier, Pete (B), Minnesota 1922
Reichardt, Bill (B), Iowa 1952
Reid, Floyd (B), Georgia 1950–56
Renner, Bill (P), Virginia Tech 1986–87
Rhodemyre, Jay (C), Kentucky 1948–52
Rice, Allen (RB), Baylor 1991
Richard, Gary (DB), Pittsburgh 1988
Riddick, Ray (E), Fordham 1940–42, 46
Ringo, Jim (C), Syracuse 1953–63
Risher, Alan (QB), Louisiana State 1987
Roach, John (QB), So. Methodist 1961–63
Robbins, Tootie (T), East Carolina 1992
Roberts, Bill (B), Dartmouth 1956
Robinson, Bill (B), Lincoln (Pa.) 1952
Robinson, Dave (LB), Penn State 1963–72
Robison, Tom (G), Texas A&M . . . . ++++1987–88
Roche, Alden (DT), Southern Univ. 1971–76
Rodgers, Del (RB), Utah . . . . #1982–84
Rohrig, Herman (B), Nebraska 1941, 46–47
Roller, Dave (DT), Kentucky 1975–78
Romine, Al (E), Alabama 1955, 58
Rosatti, Roman (T), Michigan 1924, 26–27
Rose, Al (E), Texas 1932–36
Rose, Bob (C), Ripon 1926
Rosenow, Gus (B), Wisconsin 1921
Roskie, Ken (B), South Carolina 1948
Ross, Dan (TE), Northeastern 1986
Rote, Tobin (QB), Rice 1950–56
Rowser, John (DB), Michigan 1967–69
Rubens, Larry (C), Montana State 1982–83
Rudzinski, Paul (LB), Michigan State . . 1978–81
Ruettgers, Ken (T), Southern Calif. 1985–92
Ruetz, Howard (T), Loras 1951–53

Rule, Gordon (DB), Dartmouth 1968–69
Rush, Clive (E), Miami (Ohio) 1953
Ruzich, Steve (G), Ohio State 1952–54

S

Salem, Harvey (T), California 1992
Salsbury, Jim (G), UCLA 1957–58
Sample, Chuck (B), Toledo 1942, 45
Sampson, Howard (DB), Arkansas 1978–79
Sams, Ron (G), Pittsburgh 1983
Sandifer, Dan (B), Louisiana State 1952–53
Sandusky, John (T), Villanova 1956
Sarafiny, Al (C), St. Edward's 1933
Sauer, George (B), Nebraska 1935–37
Saunders, Russ (B), Southern Calif. 1931
Scales, Hurles (DB), North Texas State . . . 1975
Schammel, Fran (G), Iowa 1937
Scherer, Bernie (E), Nebraska 1936–38
Schlinkman, Walt (B), Texas Tech 1946–50
Schmaehl, Art (B), No College 1921
Schmidt, George (C), Lewis 1952–53
Schmitt, John (C), Hofstra 1974
Schneidman, Herm (B), Iowa 1935–39
Schoemann, Roy (C), Marquette 1938
Schroll, Chuck (B), Louisiana State 1951
Schuette, Carl (B), Marquette 1950–51
Schuh, Jeff (LB), Minnesota 1986
Schuh, Harry (T), Memphis State 1974
Schultz, Charles (T), Minnesota 1939–41
Schwammel, Ade (T), Oregon St. 1934–37, 43–44
Scott, Patrick (WR), Grambling 1987–88
Scott, Randy (LB), Alabama 1981–86
Scribner, Bucky (P), Kansas 1983–84
Secord, Joe (C), No College 1922
Seeman, George (E), Nebraska 1940
Seibold, Champ (T), Wisconsin 1934–41
Self, Clarence (B), Wisconsin 1952, 54–55
Serini, Wash (G), Kentucky 1952
Shanley, Jim (B), Oregon State 1958
Sharpe, Sterling (WR), South Carolina . 1988–92
Shelly, Dexter (B), Texas 1932–33
Shield, Joe (QB), Trinity (Conn.) College 1985–86
Shirey, Fred (T), Nebraska 1940
Shumate, Mark (DE), Wisconsin 1985
Sikahema, Vai (RB/KR), Brigham Young . . 1991
Simmons, Davie (LB), North Carolina . . 1979–80
Simmons, John (DB), So. Methodist 1986
Simpkins, Ron (LB), Michigan 1988
Simpson, Nate (RB), Tennessee 1977–79
Simpson, Travis (C), Oklahoma 1987
Sims, Joe (G/T), Nebraska 1992
Singletary, Reggie (T), North Carolina St. . . 1991
Skaugstad, Daryle (NT), California 1983
Skeate, Gil (B), Gonzaga 1927
Skibinski, Joe (G), Purdue 1955–56
Skinner, Gerald (T), Arkansas 1978
Skoglund, Bob (E), Notre Dame 1947
Skoronski, Bob (T), Indiana 1956, 59–68
Sleight, Elmer (T), Purdue 1930–31
Smith, Barry (WR), Florida State 1973–75
Smith, Barty (RB), Richmond 1974–80
Smith, Ben (E), Alabama 1933
Smith, Blane (G), Purdue 1977
Smith, Bruce (B), Minnesota 1945–48
Smith, Donnell (DE), Southern Univ. 1971
Smith, Earl (T), Ripon 1922
Smith, Ed (B), New York Univ. 1937
Smith, Ernie (T), Southern Calif. 1935–37, 39
Smith, Jerry (G), Wisconsin 1956
Smith, Ollie (WR), Tennessee State 1976–77

Smith, Oscar (B), Texas Mines 1948–49
Smith, Perry (DB), Colorado State 1973–76
Smith, Red (G), Notre Dame 1927–29
Smith, Rex (E), Wisconsin Teachers 1922
Smith, Warren (C), Carleton 1921
Smith, Wes (WR), East Texas State 1987
Snelling, Ken (B), UCLA 1945
Snider, Malcolm (OL), Stanford 1972–74
Sorenson, Glen (G), Utah State 1943–45
Spagnola, John (TE), Yale 1989
Sparlis, Al (G), UCLA 1947
Spears, Ron (DE), San Diego State 1983
Spencer, Joe (T), Oklahoma A&M 1950–51
Spencer, Ollie (T), Kansas 1957–58
Spilis, John (WR), Northern Illinois 1969–71
Spinks, Jack (G), Alcorn A&M 1955–56
Sproul, Dennis (QB), Arizona State 1978

Stachowicz, Ray (P), Michigan State . . . 1981–82
Staggers, Jon (WR), Missouri 1972–74
Stahlman, Dick (E), Chicago 1931–32
Stanley, Walter (WR), Mesa State (Colo.) 1985–88
Stansauk, Don (T), Denver 1950–51
Starch, Ken (RB), Wisconsin 1976
Staroba, Paul (WR), Michigan 1973
Starr, Bart (QB), Alabama 1956–71
Starret, Ben (B), St. Mary's 1942–45
Steen, Frank (E), Rice 1939
Steiner, Rebel (E), Alabama 1950–51
Stenerud, Jan (K), Montana State 1980–83
Stephen, Scott (LB), Arizona State 1987–91
Stephenson, Dave (G), West Virginia . . . 1951–54
Sterling, John (RB), Central Oklahoma 1987
Stevens, Bill (QB), Texas-El Paso 1968–69
Stewart, Steve (LB), Minnesota 1979
Stills, Ken (DB), Wisconsin 1985–89
Stokes, Tim (T), Oregon 1978–82
Stonebraker, John (E), Southern Calif. 1942
Sturgeon, Lyle (T), North Dakota State . . . 1937
Sullivan, Carl (DE), San Jose State 1987
Sullivan, John (DB), California 1986
Sullivan, Walter (G), Beloit 1921
Summerhays, Bob (B), Utah 1949–51
Summers, Don (TE), Boise State 1987

Sutton, Mickey (CB), Montana 1989
Svendsen, Earl (C), Minnesota 1937–40
Svendsen, George (C), Minnesota 1935–41
Swanke, Karl (T/C), Boston College . . . 1980–86
Switzer, Veryl (B), Kansas State 1954–55
Sydney, Harry (FB), Kansas 1992
Symank, John (B), Florida 1957–62
Szafaryn, Len (T), North Carolina . . 1950, 53–56

T

Tagge, Jerry (QB), Nebraska 1972–74
Tassos, Damon (G), Texas A&M 1947–49
Taugher, Claude (B), Marquette 1922
Taylor, Cliff (RB), Memphis State 1976
Taylor, Jim (B), Louisiana State 1958–66
Taylor, Kitrick (WR), Washington State . . . 1992
Taylor, Lenny (WR), Tennessee 1984
Temp, Jim (E), Wisconsin 1957–60
Tenner, Bob (E), Minnesota 1935
Teteak, Deral (LB/G), Wisconsin 1952–56
Thomas, Ben (DE), Auburn . . . . ++1986–87
Thomas, Ike (DB), Bishop College 1972–73
Thomas, Lavale (RB), Fresno State 1987–88
Thomason, Bob (B), Virginia Military 1951
Thompson, Arland (G), Baylor 1981
Thompson, Aundra (WR), East Texas St. 1977–81
Thompson, Clarence (B), Minnesota 1939
Thompson, Darrell (RB), Minnesota . . . 1990–92
Thompson, John (TE), Utah State 1979–82
Thurston, Fred (G), Valparaiso 1959–67
Timberlake, George (C), Southern Calif. . . . 1955
Tinker, Gerald (WR), Kent State 1975
Tinsley, Pete (G), Georgia 1938–45
Toburen, Nelson (LB), Wichita State . . . 1961–62
Tollefson, Chuck (G), Iowa 1944–46
Tomczak, Mike (QB), Ohio State 1991
Toner, Tom (LB), Idaho State 1973–77
Tonnemaker, Clayton (LB/C),
         Minnesota 1950, 53–54
Torkelson, Eric (RB), Connecticut . . . ***1974–81
Troup, Bill (QB), South Carolina 1980
Tuaolo, Esera (NT/DE), Oregon State . . 1991–92
Tullis, Walter (WR), Delaware State . . . 1978–79
Tunnell, Emlen (B), Iowa 1959–61
Turner, Maurice (RB), Utah State 1985
Turner, Rich (DT), Oklahoma 1981–83
Turner, Wylie (DB), Angelo State 1979–80
Turpin, Miles (LB), California 1986
Tuttle, Dick (E), Minnesota 1927
Twedell, Fran (G), Minnesota 1939

U

Uecker, Keith (G/T), Auburn . . . . +1984–91
Uram, Andy (B), Minnesota 1938–43
Urban, Alex (E), South Carolina 1941, 44–45
Usher, Ed (B), Michigan 1922–24

V

Vairo, Dominic (E), Notre Dame 1935
VanderSea, Phil (B/LB),
         Massachusetts 1966, 68–70
Van Dyke, Bruce (G), Missouri 1974–76
Van Every, Hal (B), Minnesota 1940–41
Vanoy, Vernon (DL), Kansas 1972
Van Sickle, Clyde (C), Arkansas 1932–33
VantHull, Fred (G), Minnesota 1942
Van Valkenburg, Pete (RB), Brigham Young 1974
Vataha, Randy (WR), Stanford 1977
Vegara, George (E), Notre Dame 1925
Veingrad, Alan (T), East Texas St. ++++1986–90
Vereen, Carl (T), Georgia Tech 1957
Viaene, David (T), Minnesota-Duluth 1992
Villanucci, Vince (NT), Bowling Green . . . 1987
Vogds, Evan (G), Wisconsin 1948–49
Voss, Lloyd (T), Nebraska 1964–65
Voss, Walter (E), Detroit 1924

W

Wagner, Bryan (P), Cal St.-Northridge . . . 1992
Wagner, Buffton (B), Northern Michigan . . 1921
Wagner, Steve (DB), Wisconsin 1976–79
Walker, Cleo (C/LB), Louisville 1970
Walker, Malcolm (C), Rice 1970
Walker, Randy (P), Northwestern (La.) St. . 1974
Walker, Val Joe (B), So. Methodist 1953–56
Wallace, Calvin (DE), West Virginia Tech . . 1987
Walsh, Ward (RB), Tennessee 1972–73
Washington, Chuck (DB), Arkansas 1987
Watts, Elbert (DB), Southern Calif. . . ++1986–87
Weathers, Clarence (WR), Delaware St. 1990–91
Weatherwax, Jim (T), Cal St.-L.A. 1966–69
Weaver, Gary (LB), Fresno State 1975–79
Webb, Chuck (RB), Tennessee 1991
Webber, Howard (E), Kansas State 1928
Webster, Tim (K), Arkansas 1971
Weddington, Mike (LB), Oklahoma . . . 1986–90
Wehba, Ray (E), Southern Calif. 1944
Weigel, Lee (RB), Wisconsin-Eau Claire . . 1987
Weisgerber, Dick (B), Williamette . . 1938–40, 42
Weishuhn, Clayton (LB), Angelo State . . . 1987
Wellman, Mike (C), Kansas 1979–80
Wells, Don (E), Georgia 1946–49
Wells, Terry (RB), Southern Miss. 1975
West, Ed (TE), Auburn 1984–92
West, Pat (B), Southern Calif. 1948
Wheeler, Lyle (E), Ripon 1921–23
Whitaker, Bill (DB), Missouri 1981–82
White, Adrian (S), Florida 1992
White, Gene (B), Georgia 1954
Whitehurst, David (QB), Furman 1977–83
Whittenton, Jesse (B), Texas Western . . . 1958–64
Widby, Ron (P), Tennessee 1972
Wildung, Dick (T), Minnesota 1946–51, 53
Wilkins, Ted (E), Indiana 1925
Willhite, Kevin (RB), Oregon 1987
Williams, A.D. (E), Pacific 1959
Williams, Clarence (DE),
         Prairie View A&M 1970–77
Williams, Delvin (RB), Kansas 1981
Williams, Dick (B), Wisconsin 1921
Williams, Howard (B), Howard 1962–63

Williams, Perry (RB), Purdue 1969–73
Williams, Travis (HB), Arizona State . . . 1967–70
Wilson, Ben (FB), Southern Calif. 1967
Wilson, Charles (WR), Memphis State . . 1990–91
Wilson, Faye (B), Texas A&M 1931
Wilson, Gene (E), So. Methodist 1947–48
Wilson, John (B), Dubuque 1939
Wilson, Marcus (RB), Virginia 1992
Wilson, Milt (T), Wisconsin Teachers 1921
Wimberly, Abner (E), Louisiana State . . 1950–52
Wingle, Blake (G), UCLA 1985
Wingo, Rich (LB), Alabama ***1979–84
Winkler, Francis (DE), Memphis State . . 1968–69
Winkler, Randy (G), Tarleton State 1971
Winslow, Paul (E), North Carolina College 1960
Winter, Blaise (DL), Syracuse 1988–90
Winters, Arnold (T), No College 1941
Winters, Chet (RB), Oklahoma 1983
Winters, Frank (C/G), Western Illinois . . . 1992
Winther, Wimpy (C), Mississippi 1971
Withrow, Cal (C), Kentucky 1971–73
Witte, Earl (B), Gustavus Adolphus 1934
Wizbicki, Alex (B), Holy Cross 1950
Wood, Willie (S), Southern Calif. 1960–71
Woodin, Whitey (G), Marquette 1922–31
Woods, Jerry (S), Northern Michigan 1990
Woodside, Keith (RB), Texas A&M 1988–91
Workman, Vince (RB), Ohio State 1989–92
Wortman, Keith (G), Nebraska 1972–75
Wright, Randy (QB), Wisconsin 1984–88
Wright, Steve (T), Alabama 1964–66
Wunsch, Harry (G), Notre Dame 1934

Y

Young, Bill (G), Ohio State 1929
Young, Glenn (B), Purdue 1956–57
Young, Paul (C), Oklahoma 1933
Young, Steve (T), Colorado 1979

Z

Zarnas, Gus (G), Ohio State 1939–40
Zatkoff, Roger (LB), Michigan 1953–56
Zeller, Joe (G), Indiana 1932
Zendejas, Max (K), Arizona 1987–88
Zimmerman, Don (WR), Northeast La. . . . 1976
Zoll, Carl (G), No College 1921–22
Zoll, Dick (G), Indiana 1939
Zoll, Martin (G), No College 1921
Zorn, Jim (QB), Cal Poly-Pomona 1985
Zuidmulder, Dave (B), St. Ambrose 1929–31
Zupek, Al (E), Lawrence 1946
Zuver, Merle (C), Nebraska 1930

    *   not active in 1978
   **   on injured reserve in 1979
  ***   on injured reserve in 1980
 ****   on injured reserve in 1982
    #   on injured reserve in 1983
   ##   on injured reserve in 1984
  ###   on injured reserve in 1986
 ####   on injured reserve in 1986 and 1988
    +   on injured reserve in 1986 and 1989
   ++   on injured reserve in 1987
  +++   on injured reserve in 1987 and 1989
 ++++   on injured reserve in 1988
    •   on injured reserve in 1989
   ••   on reserve/non–football injury in 1989
             and injured reserve in 1990
  •••   on reserve/PUP in 1990
 ••••   on reserve/non–football illness in 1992
    &   on injured reserve in 1992

Packer Super Bowl Records

Most Games Won
2, Green Bay,
1967 vs. Kansas City, 35–10
1968 vs. Oakland, 33–14

Most Points Scored, Game
35, vs. Kansas City, 1967

Most TDs Scored, Game
5, vs. Kansas City, 1967

Fewest Points Allowed, Game
10, vs. Kansas City, 1967

Most Points, Second Half
21, vs. Kansas City, 1967

Most Points, Third Quarter
14, vs. Kansas City, 1967

Most (Net) Yards Gained, Game
358, vs. Kansas City, 1967

Fewest (Net) Yards Allowed, Game
239, vs. Kansas City, 1967

RUSHING

Most Yards, Team, Game
160, vs. Oakland, 1968
130, vs. Kansas City, 1967

Most Attempts, Individual, Game
17, Ben Wilson, 1968 vs. Oakland
16, Jim Taylor, 1967 vs. Kansas City

Most Yards, Individual, Game
65, Ben Wilson, 1968 vs. Oakland
53, Jim Taylor, 1967 vs. Kansas City

Touchdowns, Rushing, Game
**2, Elijah Pitts, 1967 vs. Kansas City

Fewest Yards Allowed Rushing, Game
72, Kansas City, 1967

Fewest TDs Allowed Rushing, Game
**0, vs. Kansas City, 1967
**0, vs. Oakland, 1968

Most Touchdowns, Game
3, vs. Kansas City, 1967

SCORING

Most Points, Game
15, Don Chandler, 1968 vs. Oakland
    (4 FGs, 3 PATs)
12, Max McGee, 1967 vs. Kansas City
    (2 TDs)
12, Elijah Pitts, 1967 vs. Kansas City
    (2 TDs)

Most Points After Touchdown, Game
5, Don Chandler, 1967 vs. Kansas City

Most Field Goals, Game
4, Don Chandler, 1968 vs. Oakland

Most Points After Touchdown, Career
**8, Don Chandler, 2 games (8 attempts)

Most Points, Career
20, Don Chandler, 2 games
    (4 FGs, 8 PATs)

PASSING

Most Yards, Team
250, vs. Kansas City, 1967

Most Attempts, Game
24, Bart Starr, vs. Oakland, 1968
23, Bart Starr, vs. Kansas City, 1967

Most Completions, Game
16, Bart Starr, vs. Kansas City, 1967

Most Yardage, Individual
250, Bart Starr, vs. Kansas City, 1967

Most Touchdowns, Game
2, Bart Starr, 1967 vs. Kansas City

Interceptions, Game
1, Bart Starr, 1967 vs. Kansas City
    (23 attempts)

**Lowest Percentage, Passes Had
Intercepted, Career**
2.13, Bart Starr, Green Bay, 2 games (47–1)

RECEIVING

Most Passes Caught, Game
7, Max McGee, 1967 vs. Kansas City

Most Yards Gained, Game
138, Max McGee, 1967 vs. Kansas City
    (7 receptions)
71, Boyd Dowler, 1968 vs. Oakland
    (2 receptions)

Most Yards Gained, Career
171, Max McGee, 2 games

Most TD Passes, Game
**2, Max McGee, 1967 vs. Kansas City

PUNTING

Most Punts, Game
6, Donny Anderson, 1968 vs. Oakland
3, Don Chandler, 1967 vs. Kansas City

Highest Average, Game
43.3, Don Chandler, 1967 vs. Kansas City

PUNT RETURNS

Most Punts Returned, Game
5, Willie Wood, 1968 vs. Oakland
3, Donny Anderson, 1967 vs. Kansas City

Most Yards Gained, Game
35, Willie Wood, 1968 vs. Oakland
25, Donny Anderson, 1967 vs. Kansas City

Longest Punt Returns
31, Willie Wood, 1968 vs. Oakland
15, Donny Anderson 1967 vs. Kansas City

Most Punts Returned, Team, Game
5, Green Bay vs. Oakland, 1968

Most Punt Returns, Career
6, Willie Wood, 2 games

KICKOFF RETURNS

Most Kickoffs Returned, Game
2, Herb Adderley, 1967 vs. Kansas City

Most Yards Gained, Game
40, Herb Adderley, 1967 vs. Kansas City

Longest Kickoff Returns
25, Donny Anderson, 1967 vs. Kansas City

INTERCEPTIONS

Most Interceptions, Game
1, Willie Wood, 1967 vs. Kansas City
1, Herb Adderley, 1968 vs. Oakland

Most Interception Return Yards, Game
60, Herb Adderley, 1968 vs. Oakland
50, Willie Wood, 1967 vs. Kansas City

Longest Interception Returns
60, Herb Adderley, 1968 vs. Oakland

Most Touchdowns
**1, Herb Adderley, 1968 vs. Oakland

**Shares Super Bowl Record

Packer All-Time Record 1921-1992

	OVERALL RECORD				HOME GREEN BAY			MILWAUKEE			AWAY		
Year	W	L	T	Pct.	W	L	T	W	L	T	W	L	T
1921	3	2	1	.600	3	1	0	-	-	-	0	1	1
1922	4	3	3	.571	3	1	1	-	-	-	*1	2	2
1923	7	2	1	.778	4	2	1	-	-	-	3	0	0
1924	7	4	0	.636	5	0	0	-	-	-	2	4	0
1925	8	5	0	.615	6	0	0	-	-	-	2	5	0
1926	7	3	3	.700	4	1	2	-	-	-	3	2	1
1927	7	2	1	.778	6	1	0	-	-	-	1	1	1
1928	6	4	3	.600	3	2	2	-	-	-	3	2	1
1929	12	0	1	1.000	5	0	0	-	-	-	7	0	1
1930	10	3	1	.769	6	0	0	-	-	-	4	3	1
1931	12	2	0	.857	8	0	0	-	-	-	4	2	0
1932	10	3	1	.769	5	0	1	-	-	-	5	3	0
1933	5	7	1	.417	3	1	1	0	1	0	2	5	0
1934	7	6	0	.538	3	2	0	1	1	0	3	3	0
1935	8	4	0	.667	4	1	0	1	1	0	3	2	0
1936	10	1	1	.909	3	1	0	2	0	0	5	0	1
1937	7	4	0	.636	2	2	0	2	0	0	3	2	0
1938	8	3	0	.727	2	2	0	2	0	0	*4	1	0
1939	9	2	0	.818	3	1	0	2	0	0	4	1	0
1940	6	4	1	.600	2	2	0	2	0	0	2	2	1
1941	10	1	0	.909	2	1	0	3	0	0	5	0	0
1942	8	2	1	.800	2	1	0	2	0	0	4	1	1
1943	7	2	1	.778	1	0	1	1	1	0	5	1	0
1944	8	2	0	.800	3	0	0	2	0	0	3	2	0
1945	6	4	0	.600	2	1	0	2	0	0	2	3	0
1946	6	5	0	.545	1	2	0	1	1	0	4	2	0
1947	6	5	1	.545	2	1	0	2	1	0	2	3	1
1948	3	9	0	.250	2	1	0	0	3	0	1	5	0
1949	2	10	0	.167	0	3	0	1	2	0	1	5	0
1950	3	9	0	.250	2	2	0	1	1	0	0	6	0
1951	3	9	0	.250	1	3	0	1	1	0	1	5	0
1952	6	6	0	.500	1	2	0	2	1	0	3	3	0
1953	2	9	1	.182	1	2	0	0	3	0	1	4	1
1954	4	8	0	.333	0	3	0	2	1	0	2	4	0
1955	6	6	0	.500	3	0	0	2	1	0	1	5	0
1956	4	8	0	.333	0	3	0	2	1	0	2	4	0
1957	3	9	0	.250	1	2	0	0	3	0	2	4	0
1958	1	10	1	.091	1	2	1	0	2	0	0	6	0
1959	7	5	0	.583	4	0	0	0	2	0	3	3	0
1960	8	4	0	.667	3	1	0	1	1	0	4	2	0

	OVERALL RECORD				HOME GREEN BAY			MILWAUKEE			AWAY		
Year	W	L	T	Pct.	W	L	T	W	L	T	W	L	T
1961	11	3	0	.786	4	0	0	2	1	0	5	2	0
1962	13	1	0	.929	4	0	0	3	0	0	6	1	0
1963	11	2	1	.846	3	1	0	3	0	0	5	1	1
1964	8	5	1	.615	2	2	0	2	1	0	4	2	1
1965	10	3	1	.769	3	1	0	3	0	0	4	2	1
1966	12	2	0	.857	3	1	0	3	0	0	6	1	0
1967	9	4	1	.692	2	1	1	2	1	0	5	2	0
1968	6	7	1	.462	1	3	0	1	2	0	4	2	1
1969	8	6	0	.571	3	1	0	2	1	0	3	4	0
1970	6	8	0	.429	2	2	0	2	1	0	2	5	0
1971	4	8	2	.333	2	2	0	1	1	1	1	5	1
1972	10	4	0	.714	2	2	0	2	1	0	6	1	0
1973	5	7	2	.429	1	2	1	2	0	1	2	5	0
1974	6	8	0	.429	1	3	0	3	0	0	2	5	0
1975	4	10	0	.286	2	2	0	1	2	0	1	6	0
1976	5	9	0	.357	2	2	0	2	1	0	1	6	0
1977	4	10	0	.286	1	3	0	1	2	0	2	5	0
1978	8	7	1	.531	2	1	1	3	1	0	3	5	0
1979	5	11	0	.313	1	4	0	3	0	0	1	7	0
1980	5	10	1	.344	3	1	0	1	3	0	1	6	1
1981	8	8	0	.500	3	2	0	1	2	0	4	4	0
1982	5	3	1	.611	0	1	0	3	0	0	2	2	1
1983	8	8	0	.500	3	2	0	2	1	0	3	5	0
1984	8	8	0	.500	3	2	0	2	1	0	3	5	0
1985	8	8	0	.500	3	2	0	2	1	0	3	5	0
1986	4	12	0	.250	0	5	0	1	2	0	3	5	0
1987	5	9	1	.367	1	4	0	1	1	1	3	4	0
1988	4	12	0	.250	1	4	0	1	2	0	2	6	0
1989	10	6	0	.625	3	2	0	3	0	0	4	4	0
1990	6	10	0	.375	1	4	0	2	1	0	3	5	0
1991	4	12	0	.250	1	4	0	1	2	0	2	6	0
1992	9	7	0	.563	3	2	0	3	0	0	3	5	0
Totals	485	415	36	.537	178	118	13	101	59	3	#206	238	20

* includes one neutral site victory

\# includes two neutral site victories

The Green Bay Packers own a 485–415–36 regular-season record in their 72 seasons of play in the National Football League (1921–92) — a .537 winning percentage.

The Packers are 178–118–13 (.597) in Green Bay and 101–59–3 (.629) in Milwaukee for an overall home mark of 279–177–16 (.608). The Packers first began to play league games in Milwaukee on an annual basis in 1933.

On the road, Green Bay stands 206–238–20 (.466), a mark which includes two neutral site contests.

The Packers played independent football during the 1919–20 seasons.

Past Head Coaches

Earl "Curly" Lambeau
1921–1949
Coaching Record: 212–106–21
Winning Pct.: .656

Gene Ronzani
1950–1953
Coaching Record: 14–31–1
Winning Pct.: .315

Lisle Blackbourn
19 54–1957
Coaching Record: 17–31–0
Winning Pct.: .354

***Ray "Scooter" McLean**
1958
Coaching Record: 1–10–1
Winning Pct.: .125

Vince Lombardi
1959–1967
Coaching Record: 98–30–4
Winning Pct.: .758

Phil Bengtson
1968–1970
Coaching Record: 20–21–1
Winning Pct.: .488

Dan Devine
1971–1974
Coaching Record: 25–28–4
Winning Pct.: .474

Bart Starr
1975–1983
Coaching Record: 53–77–3
Winning Pct.: .410

Forrest Gregg
1984–1987
Coaching Record: 25–37–1
Winning Pct.: .405

Lindy Infante
1988–1991
Coaching Record: 24–40–0
Winning Pct.: .375

* McLean and Hugh Devore also served as co-head coaches for last 2 games of 1953 season and had a joint 0–2 record.

Packer All-Time Teams

1946

Don Hutson	End
Robert "Cal" Hubbard	Tackle
Mike Michalske	Guard
Charley Brock	Center
Charles "Buckets" Goldenberg	Guard
Howard "Cub" Buck	Tackle
LaVern "Lavvie" Dilweg	End
Arnold Herber	Quarterback
Johnny Blood	Halfback
Verne Lewellen	Halfback
Clarke Hinkle	Fullback

1957

Don Hutson	End
Robert "Cal" Hubbard	Tackle
Mike Michalske	Guard
Charley Brock	Center
Charles "Buckets" Goldenberg	Guard
Howard "Cub" Buck	Tackle
LaVern "Lavvie" Dilweg	End
Arnold Herber	Quarterback
Johnny Blood	Halfback
Tony Canadeo	Halfback
Clarke Hinkle	Fullback

1969
(50th Anniversary All-Time Packer Team)

OFFENSE

Don Hutson	End
Boyd Dowler	End
Robert "Cal" Hubbard	Tackle
Fred "Fuzzy" Thurston	Guard
Jim Ringo	Center
Jerry Kramer	Guard
Forrest Gregg	Tackle
Bart Starr	Quarterback
Paul Hornung	Running Back
Clarke Hinkle	Running Back
Jim Taylor	Running Back

DEFENSE

Larry Craig	End
LaVern "Lavvie" Dilweg	End
Willie Davis	End
Robert "Cal" Hubbard	Tackle
Henry Jordan	Tackle
Dave Hanner	Tackle
Ray Nitschke	Linebacker
Dave Robinson	Linebacker
Bill Forester	Linebacker
Herb Adderley	Defensive Back
Jess Whittenton	Defensive Back
Bobby Dillon	Defensive Back
Willie Wood	Defensive Back

1976
(Iron Man and Modern Era All-Time Packer Teams)

IRON MAN ERA TEAM

Don Hutson	End
Milt Gantenbein	End
Robert "Cal" Hubbard	Tackle
Mike Michalske	Guard
Charley Brock	Center
Charles "Buckets" Goldenberg	Guard

Buford "Baby" Ray	Tackle
Larry Craig	Blocking Back
Johnny Blood	Halfback
Tony Canadeo	Halfback
Clarke Hinkle	Fullback

MODERN ERA TEAM

OFFENSE

Boyd Dowler	Wide Receiver
Bob Skoronski	Tackle
Fred "Fuzzy" Thurston	Guard
Jim Ringo	Center
Jerry Kramer	Guard
Forrest Gregg	Tackle
Ron Kramer	Tight End
Max McGee	Wide Receiver
Bart Starr	Quarterback
Paul Hornung	Running Back
Jim Taylor	Running Back

DEFENSE

Willie Davis	End
Henry Jordan	Tackle
Dave Hanner	Tackle
Lionel Aldridge	End
Dave Robinson	Left Linebacker
Ray Nitschke	Middle Linebacker
Fred Carr	Right Linebacker
Herb Adderley	Left Cornerback
Bob Jeter	Right Cornerback
Willie Wood	Safety
Bobby Dillon	Safety

Specialists

Dick Deschaine	Punter
Don Chandler	Placekicker

*Iron Man and Modern Era Teams were chosen by a vote of fans from
29 states in 1976 Packer game program poll.*

Team Records

YARDS GAINED

Most Yards Gained (season)
6,172, 1983 (1,807 rushing, 4,365 passing)
5,780, 1989 (1,732 rushing, 4,048 passing)
5,449, 1984 (2,019 rushing, 3,430 passing)
5,371, 1985 (2,208 rushing, 3,163 passing)
5,097, 1980 (1,806 rushing, 3,291 passing)
5,061, 1986 (1,614 rushing, 3,447 passing)
4,859, 1981 (1,670 rushing, 3,189 passing)
4,791, 1962 (2,460 rushing, 2,331 passing)

Most Gross Yards Passing (season)
4,688, 1983   3,651, 1980
4,325, 1989   3,609, 1988
3,740, 1984   3,576, 1981
3,708, 1986   3,552, 1985
3,696, 1990   3,498, 1992

Most Net Yards Passing (season)
4,365, 1983   3,291, 1980
4,048, 1989   3,285, 1988
3,447, 1986   3,230, 1992
3,430, 1984   3,189, 1981
3,306, 1990   3,163, 1985

Most Net Yards Gained Passing (game)
423, vs. Chicago Cardinals, Nov. 1, 1942 (27 att., 13 comp., 6 TDs, 1 INT)
422, vs. St. Louis, Dec. 21, 1969 (34 att., 23 comp., 5 TDs, 1 INT)
415, vs. Tampa Bay, Oct. 12, 1980 (51 att., 35 comp., 1 TD, 2 INTs)
403, vs. Washington, Oct. 17, 1983 (32 att., 23 comp., 3 TDs, 1 INT)

Fewest Net Yards Gained Passing (game)
–35, vs. Cincinnati, Sept. 26, 1976
–12, vs. Chicago, Nov. 4, 1973
–10, vs. Dallas, Oct. 24, 1965
–2, vs. Detroit, Nov. 7, 1965

Most Yards Gained Rushing (season)
2,460, 1962   2,248, 1963
2,350, 1961   2,227, 1971
2,276, 1964

Most Yards Gained Rushing (game)
366, vs. Detroit, Oct. 26, 1947 (50 attempts)
312, vs. New York Yanks, Oct. 8, 1950 (40 attempts)
303, vs. Baltimore, Oct. 18, 1953 (56 attempts)
301, at Washington, Dec. 1, 1946 (64 attempts)
298, at Chicago, Dec. 16, 1973 (53 attempts)
294, vs. Cleveland Rams, Oct. 22, 1944 (45 attempts)
294, at Philadelphia, Nov. 11, 1962 (55 attempts)

288, vs. Pittsburgh, Oct. 20, 1946 (63 attempts)
285, vs. Detroit, Oct. 6, 1985 (47 attempts)
284, vs. San Francisco, Oct. 11, 1959 (55 attempts)

Most Yards Gained (game)
628, at Philadelphia, Nov. 11, 1962 (294 rushing, 334 passing)

Most Rushing Attempts, Both Teams (game)
108, GB (38) at Chicago Cardinals (70), Dec. 5, 1948
102, GB (51) vs. Pittsburgh (51), Nov. 20, 1949

Fewest Rushing Attempts (game)
10, vs. Seattle, Dec. 9, 1990
11, at Chicago, Nov. 27, 1988
12, vs. San Diego, Oct. 7, 1984
13, at Tampa Bay, Oct. 14, 1990
13, vs. Philadelphia, Sept. 1, 1991
13, at Minnesota, Dec. 27, 1992

Most Touchdowns Rushing (season)
*36, 1962 (14 games)
29, 1960 (12 games)

Most Seasons Leading League
4 (1946, 1961–62, 1964)

Fewest Yards Rushing (game)
13, vs. Seattle, Dec. 9, 1990 (10 attempts)
17, vs. Boston Redskins, Sept. 17, 1933 (37 attempts)
18, vs. Chicago Cardinals, Oct. 21, 1934 (29 attempts)
20, at Boston Redskins, Nov. 8, 1936 (30 attempts)
20, at Baltimore, Oct. 28, 1956 (18 attempts)
22, at Los Angeles Rams, Nov. 28, 1965 (16 attempts)
22, at Chicago, Nov. 27, 1988 (11 attempts)

FIRST DOWNS

Seasons Leading League
5 (1940, 1942, 1944, 1960, 1962)

Most First Downs (season)
342, 1989 (114 rushing, 207 passing, 21 penalty)
340, 1983 (99 rushing, 214 passing, 27 penalty)
318, 1985 (114 rushing, 172 passing, 32 penalty)
315, 1984 (120 rushing, 168 passing, 27 penalty)

308, 1981 (104 rushing, 174 passing, 30 penalty)
307, 1980 (119 rushing, 164 passing, 24 penalty)
291, 1992 (101 rushing, 171 passing, 19 penalty)
286, 1986 (96 rushing, 172 passing, 18 penalty)
281, 1962 (151 rushing, 114 passing, 16 penalty)
280, 1988 (77 rushing, 176 passing, 27 penalty)

Most First Downs (game)
37, at Philadelphia, Nov. 11, 1962 (21 rushing, 15 passing, 1 penalty)
32, at Tampa Bay, Oct. 12, 1980 (11 rushing, 21 passing)
31, vs. Tampa Bay, Dec. 1, 1985 (12 rushing, 17 passing, 2 penalty)
31, at Detroit, Nov. 12, 1989 (10 rushing, 19 passing, 2 penalty)
30, vs. Detroit, Oct. 28, 1984 (10 rushing, 16 passing, 4 penalty)
30, vs. Detroit, Oct. 6, 1985 (16 rushing, 13 passing, 1 penalty)
29, at Minnesota, Oct. 14, 1962 (13 rushing, 15 passing, 3 penalty)
29, vs. San Francisco, Oct. 26, 1986 (17 rushing, 12 passing)
29, vs. New Orleans, Sept. 17, 1989 (10 rushing, 18 passing, 1 penalty)
29, at Los Angeles Rams, Sept. 24, 1989 (9 rushing, 16 passing, 4 penalty)

Fewest First Downs to Opponent (game)
*0, vs. New York Giants, Oct. 1, 1933

Fewest First Downs, Both Teams (game)
5, GB (5) vs. New York Giants (0), Oct. 1, 1933

FORWARD PASSING

Most Passes Completed (season)
354, 1989 (600 attempts)   311, 1983 (526 attempts)
340, 1992 (527 attempts)   305, 1986 (565 attempts)
319, 1988 (582 attempts)

Most Passes Attempted (season)
600, 1989 (354 completed)   565, 1986 (305 completed)
582, 1988 (319 completed)   541, 1990 (302 completed)

Most Passes Attempted (game)
60, at Detroit, Nov. 12, 1989 (35 completed)
59, at New Orleans, Sept. 14, 1986 (28 completed)
57, vs. San Francisco, Oct. 26, 1986 (32 completed)
56, at Los Angeles Rams, Dec. 16, 1951 (27 completed)
Best Passing Efficiency (season – 250 minimum)
64.5%, 1992 (340 completions in 527 attempts)
60.7%, 1966 (193 completions in 318 attempts)
60.1%, 1962 (187 completions in 311 attempts)
59.1%, 1968 (188 completions in 318 attempts)
59.1%, 1983 (311 completions in 526 attempts)

Fewest Passes Attempted (game)
*0, vs. Portsmouth, Oct. 8, 1933

Seasons Leading League, Passing Yardage
Fewest Yards Gained Passing, Both Teams (game)
*–11, GB (–10) vs. Dallas (–1), Oct. 24, 1965

Most Touchdown Passes (season)
33, 1983   27, 1989
30, 1984   26, 1951
28, 1942   26, 1952

Most Touchdown Passes (game)
6, vs. Chicago Cardinals, Nov. 1, 1942
6, vs. Detroit, Oct. 7, 1945

Most Passes Had Intercepted (game)
8, vs. New York Giants, Nov. 21, 1948
7, vs. Chicago Bears, Sept. 22, 1940
7, vs. Detroit, Oct. 20, 1940
7, vs. Detroit, Sept. 17, 1950

Most Times Sacked (game)
11, vs. Detroit, Nov. 7, 1965

Most Times Sacked, Both Teams (game)
*18, GB (10) at San Diego (8), Sept. 24, 1978

Fewest Quarterback Sacks Allowed (season)
17, 1972 (14 games)
17, 1974 (14 games)

Fewest Yards Allowed by Quarterback Sacks (season)
104, 1972
126, 1974

Most Seasons Leading League, Completion Percentage
7 (1936, 1941, 1961–62, 1964, 1966, 1968)

Fewest Passes Had Intercepted (season)
*5, 1966 (318 attempts)
6, 1964 (321 attempts)

Most Passes Had Intercepted, Both Teams (game)
11, GB (4) at Cleveland Rams (7), Oct. 30, 1938
11, GB (7) vs. Detroit (4), Oct. 20, 1940

Most Seasons Leading League, Net Yards Gained Rushing and Passing
3 (1937–38, 1940)

SCORING

Most Touchdowns (season)
53, 1962 (14 games)   44, 1931 (14 games)
52, 1983 (16 games)   44, 1964 (14 games)
51, 1984 (16 games)   43, 1966 (14 games)
49, 1961 (14 games)   42, 1989 (16 games)
46, 1963 (14 games)

Most Touchdowns Rushing (season)
*36, 1962 (14 games)   23, 1964 (14 games)
29, 1960 (12 games)   22, 1963 (14 games)
27, 1961 (14 games)

Most Points After Touchdown (season)
52, 1962 (53 attempts)   42, 1964 (44 att.)
52, 1983 (52 att.)   42, 1989 (42 att.)
49, 1961 (49 att.)   41, 1960 (41 att.)
48, 1984 (50 att.)   41, 1966 (43 att.)
43, 1963 (46 att.)

Most Seasons Leading League, Touchdowns
5 (1932, 1937–38, 1961–62)

Most Field Goals (season)
33, 1972 (48 att.)   22, 1992 (29 att.)
25, 1974 (39 att.)   21, 1973 (35 att.)
23, 1990 (30 att.)   21, 1983 (26 att.)
22, 1981 (24 att.)   19, 1967 (26 att.)
22, 1989 (28 att.)   19, 1985 (26 att.)

Most Points (season)
429, 1983 (16 games)   369, 1963 (14 games)
415, 1962 (14 games)   362, 1989 (16 games)
391, 1961 (14 games)   342, 1964 (14 games)
390, 1984 (16 games)

Fewest Points (season)
80, 1922 (11 games)   113, 1927 (10 games)
85, 1923 (10 games)   114, 1949 (12 games)
108, 1924 (11 games)

Most Points Scored (game)
57, vs. Detroit, Oct. 7, 1945 (57–21)
56, vs. Atlanta, Oct. 23, 1966 (56–3)
55, vs. Chicago Cardinals, Nov. 1, 1942 (55–24)
55, vs. Cleveland, Nov. 12, 1967 (55–7)
55, vs. Tampa Bay, Oct. 2, 1983 (55–14)

Most Points, Both Teams (game)
95, GB (48) vs. Washington (47), Oct. 17, 1983
88, GB (41) at Atlanta (47), Nov. 27, 1983 (ot)
87, GB (35) at Detroit (52), Nov. 22, 1951
84, GB (44) at Detroit (40), Nov. 27, 1986
83, GB (31) at Chicago Bears (52), Nov. 6, 1955

Most Points (one team, one quarter)
*41, GB vs. Detroit (second quarter), Oct. 7, 1945
35, GB vs. Cleveland (first quarter), Nov. 12, 1967
35, GB vs. Tampa Bay (second quarter), Oct. 2, 1983

Most Points (one team, one half)
*49, GB vs. Tampa Bay (first half), Oct. 2, 1983 (55–14)
45, GB vs. Cleveland (first half), Nov. 12, 1967 (55–7)

Most Touchdowns Rushing (game)
6, at Pittsburgh, Nov. 23, 1941
6, at Cleveland, Oct. 15, 1961
6, at Philadelphia, Nov. 11, 1962

Most Field Goals Attempted (season)
48, 1972 (made 33)
39, 1974 (made 25)
35, 1973 (made 21)

Most Field Goals Attempted, Both Teams (game)
11, GB (6) vs. Detroit (5), Sept. 29, 1974

Fewest Field Goals (season — since 1932)
0, 1932
0, 1944

Most Field Goals, Both Teams (game)
8, GB (4) vs. Detroit (4), Sept. 29, 1974

Most Points After Touchdown (game)
8, vs. Atlanta, Oct. 23, 1966
7, vs. Chicago Cardinals, Nov. 1, 1942
7, vs. Detroit, Oct. 7, 1945
7, at Cleveland, Oct. 15, 1961
7, vs. Chicago Bears, Sept. 30, 1962
7, at Philadelphia, Nov. 11, 1962
7, vs. Cleveland, Nov. 12, 1967
7, vs. Tampa Bay, Oct. 2, 1983

Most Touchdowns (game)
8, vs. Chicago Cardinals, Nov. 1, 1942
8, vs. Detroit, Oct. 7, 1945
8, vs. Atlanta, Oct. 23, 1966

Fewest Points, Shutout Victory (game)
2, at Chicago Bears, Oct. 16, 1932

NFL Title Game Records

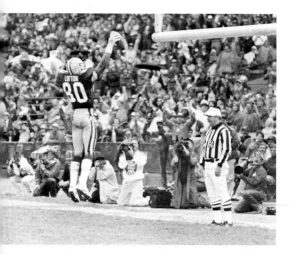

(Does Not Include AFL-NFL and AFC-NFC Title Games)

CHAMPIONSHIPS WON
*11, Green Bay (1929, '30, '31, '36, '39, '44, '61, '62, '65, '66 and '67)

RUSHING

Most Attempts — lifetime
106, Jim Taylor, 5 games

Most Attempts — game
31, Jim Taylor vs. Browns, 1965

Most Yards — lifetime
392, Jim Taylor, 5 games

Most Yards — game
105, Jim Taylor, 1960
105, Paul Hornung, 1965

PASSING

Most Attempts — lifetime
147, Bart Starr, 6 games

Most Attempts — game
35, Bart Starr, 1960 vs. Eagles

Most Completions — lifetime
84, Bart Starr, 6 games

Most Completions — game
25, Bart Starr, 1960

Most Yardage — lifetime
990 yards, Bart Starr, 6 games

Most Yardage — game
304, Bart Starr vs. Cowboys, 1966

Most Touchdowns — lifetime
11, Bart Starr, 6 games

Most Touchdowns — game
4, Bart Starr vs. Cowboys, 1966

PUNT RETURNS

Most — game
8, Green Bay vs. Giants, 1944

Most Yardage — game
89, Green Bay vs. Giants, 1944

SCORING

Most Points — game
**19, Paul Hornung, vs. Giants, 1961
(1 TD, 3 FGs, 4 PATs)

INTERCEPTIONS

Most Passes Intercepted — game
6, vs. Giants, 1939

Most Yardage, Interceptions Returned — game
123, vs. Giants, 1939 (6 int.)

Most Interceptions
3, Joe Laws vs. Giants, 1944

FIELD GOALS

Most Field Goals — team
14, Green Bay
(11 games, 19 attempts)

Most Attempted — game
5, vs. Giants, 1962

Most Field Goals — game
3, Paul Hornung vs. Giants, 1961 (3 att.)
3, Jerry Kramer vs. Giants, 1962 (5 att.)
3, Don Chandler vs. Browns, 1965 (3 att.)

DEFENSIVE RECORDS

Total Yards Allowed — game
116, vs. Boston, 1936

Yards Allowed Rushing — game
31, vs. Giants, 1961
39, vs. Boston, 1936

First Downs Allowed — game
6, vs. Giants, 1961

*League Record
**Shares League Record

PACKER RETIRED NUMBERS

3	Tony Canadeo (1952)
14	Don Hutson (1951)
15	Bart Starr (1973)
66	Ray Nitschke (1983)

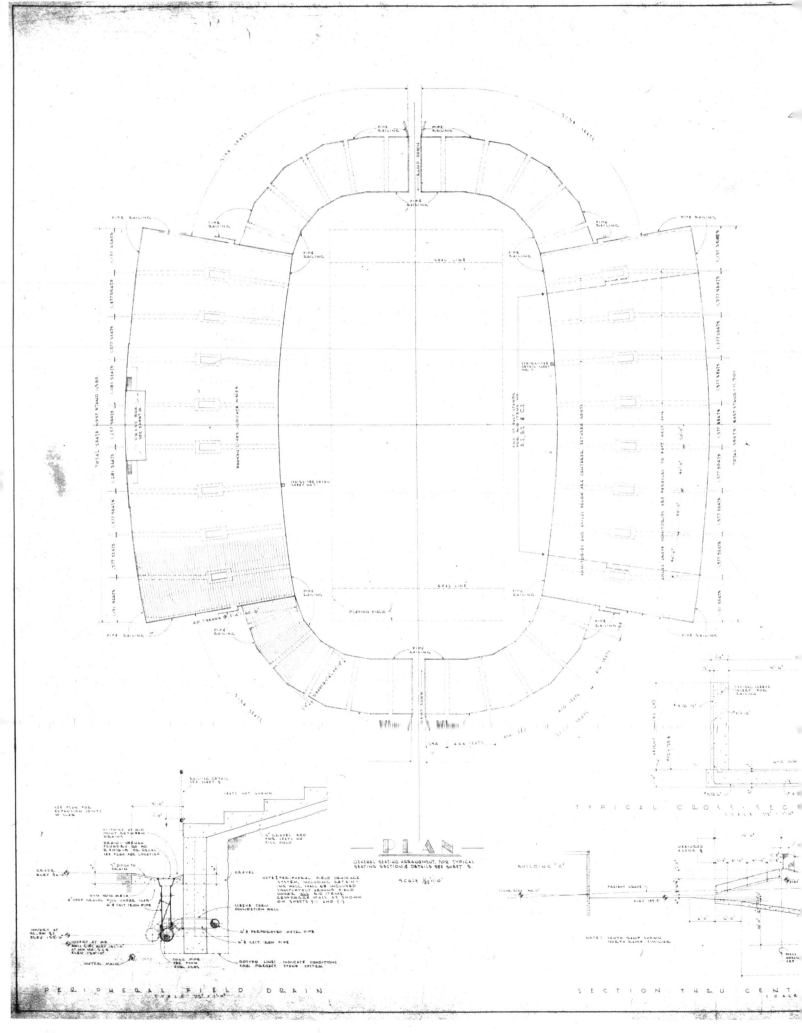